ORGANIZATIONAL SPOKESMANSHIP

SO YOU WANT TO BECOME A PRESS SECRETARY

By Daniel Walsch

George Mason University

Bassim Hamadeh, CEO and Publisher
Michael Simpson, Vice President of Acquisitions
Jamie Giganti, Managing Editor
Jess Busch, Graphic Design Supervisor
Melissa Barcomb, Acquisitions Editor
Sarah Wheeler, Project Editor
Natalie Lakosil, Licensing Associate
Sean Adams, Interior Designer

First published in the United States of America in 2014 by Cognella, Inc.

Cover image: Copyright © 2013 by Depositphotos Inc./macor.

Printed in the United States of America

ISBN: 978-1-62131-901-6 (pbk)/ 978-1-62131-902-3 (br)

www.cognella.com   800-200-3908

Contents

Chapter Two: Organizational Role

Chapter Three: Measuring Success and Effectiveness

Chapter Four: Legal and Ethical Aspects 75

Chapter Five: The Road to Spokesmanship 87

Dedication

It is not the critic who counts; not the man who points out how the strong man stumbles, or where the doer of deeds could have done them better. The credit belongs to the man who is actually in the arena, whose face is marred by dust and sweat and blood; who strives valiantly; who errs, who comes short again and again, because there is no effort without error and shortcoming; but who does actually strive to do the deeds.

—Theodore Roosevelt (1910)

I find it difficult not to view the organizational or media spokesman as being the person "in the arena" on whom Roosevelt reflected in Paris in 1910, 1 year after having completed his tenure as one of the United States' most colorful and controversial presidents. Standing unblinkingly in front of a microphone or members of the press is not the easiest thing to do. Preparing to speak with the knowledge that what you say and how you say it will be challenged, questioned, and judged by others and may very well impact the lives of those with whom you work and possibly even shape the future of that which you represent is daunting. Why would anyone want to put himself into such a predicament knowingly, regularly, and for a living?

Yet there are those who do this very thing much in the same vein as those who want to take the final shot with seconds left in the game, knowing that last-moment effort will spell the difference between victory and defeat. In the case of the spokesman, what rides on his or her "shot" is more than simple victory. When the spokesman speaks, the reputation and standing of others are affected; the ability of others to maintain employment or a lifestyle on which they depend can be in the balance. Money is at stake. Reputations are in the balance. Future courses of action may be determined—in the arena indeed.

I dedicate this book to this special breed of men and women who give their voice and intellect to the enhancement of others. I tip my hat to those who seek to advance communication in the name of strengthening ties and re-enforcing the reality that societal progress is the result of building on what we share while respectfully facing what we do not.

Introduction

It was a time unprecedented in American history. A sitting president had resigned amid great outrage and controversy. Succeeding him was his vice president, a member of the United States House of Representatives from Michigan, who had been appointed to the position only 10 months before when the then–vice president had resigned because of his own corruption challenges. The new president, liked by his colleagues but not well known among the general public, stepped into his position with caution and some trepidation. A national figure for more than 25 years, he knew well the significance of this time in the country's evolution. He also knew it was he and only he standing center stage who was about to lead a nervous nation into what many saw as unchartered territory.

Recognizing his challenge, Gerald R. Ford, the 38th president of the United States, realized he must take immediate steps to reassure the nation that its innate stability was not under siege or under any threat of compromise. To give himself a measure of comfort and to help reinsert a sense of stability into the American psyche, immediately upon taking office, Ford announced one of his first appointments: Jerald terHorst, one of the Detroit Free Press's top reporters, as press secretary. The appointment was made before Ford and his family had even been able to spend their first night at the White House. terHorst accepted with little hesitation.

The two were already well acquainted, as terHorst had been covering Ford and national politics since the late 1940s (terHorst, 1974). Though not close friends, the two had crossed paths many times over the years and had a friendly, easygoing relationship.

Also, the two held the other in high regard, as each found the other to be honest, to be straightforward-thinking, and to share similar political leanings (Kunhardt, 1999).

From the moment he accepted the appointment, terHorst had his hands full. The early days and weeks of Ford's new presidency were dominated by reports and speculation as to what Ford was going to do regarding the disgraced Richard Nixon. There was chatter that he would do nothing and simply let the courts and investigative bodies deal with the 37th president. Others speculated that Ford would go the other way and grant Nixon a blanket pardon. In his dealings with the national media and general public, press secretary terHorst repeatedly assured any and all that the president had no plans to insert himself into the Nixon matter; nor did he have any plans to grant Nixon a pardon.

Then, on September 8, 30 days after assuming office, President Ford went on national television and announced his immediate blanket pardon of President Nixon of all possible crimes relating to the Watergate scandal. The announcement caught many, particularly terHorst, by surprise. Not surprisingly, many in the nation erupted with great outrage. But one person in particular—one closer than many to the newly appointed president—was especially disturbed. Within 24 hours of President Ford's decision, terHorst handed in his resignation, claiming that as the president's primary spokesperson he could not support or defend this decision. He also suggested that the president's decision had placed him in an awkward position, as for the past month he had been telling reporters that such action by the president was not under consideration. Thus, terHorst feared that his credibility with the media and general public had been compromised. Though this was his first job as a spokesman, terHorst knew enough to know that any time the credibility of a public spokesman is damaged or compromised, such a turn of events is the equivalent of a professional kiss of death.

President Ford's controversial decision ignited much animosity toward him. Historians cite it as a key factor as to why he lost the 1976 presidential election to Jimmy Carter. One even said that terHorst's act of conscience actually trumped President Ford's (Werth, 2006). terHorst's decision to resign added fuel to a national discontent. While it did not cripple the fledgling Ford presidency, the pardon helped cast strong doubt as to Ford's ability to help lead the nation to a better place in the aftermath of the Nixon presidency. Though terHorst had the shortest tenure of any presidential press secretary in the nation's history, he continues to be cited as being among the most memorable. In 2001, he was honored for the stand he took in the Nixon case by receiving the John F. Kennedy Profile in Courage Award.

As the resignation of a sitting president was and remains unprecedented, so, too, was the action taken by terHorst. Leaders, particularly ones at such a high rung as the president of the United States, stake much of their power on a reputation that amplifies definitiveness, conviction, and confidence. When they make pronouncements or decisions, then things get done, change happens, and those around them fall into line. This was certainly the overriding perception back in 1974, at a time when rarely before had a president been openly challenged by an appointee so strongly that the staff member stepped down prior to the natural ending of his term of office. terHorst's abrupt resignation cast doubt on Ford's strength as a leader. It also, like never before, gave the American public a sharp glimpse as to the potential weight of an organization's spokesperson. Though Ford did not retract his pardon of Nixon, for the remaining time of his short-lived stint as the nation's chief executive, the action of his organizational spokesman remained a bruise that never disappeared.

In the nearly 40 years since that volatile time, presidential press secretaries certainly have come and gone. Despite that, the importance of this position within our government's top administration has not decreased. Organizations, whether they are at the top level of the federal government or in the private sector, are inherently engaged in rhetoric, and their rhetoric is inherently tied to their organization (Crable, 2004). Their actions, specifically designed to help their employer provide various services or turn a profit, represent forms of communication that define the essence of the entity. Thus, a role to help facilitate this ongoing communicating or dialogue is needed. Often, as in the case of a president's press secretary, it is here where the organizational spokesperson fits in. This professional is highly influential. Day in and day out, the national press and general public are subject to the regular briefings of this person more than those of any other top official. Depending on what he or she has to share, lead stories on all news outlets are influenced or determined, other elected officials shape their actions, and even other governments consider policy. This professional continues to serve as a direct line between the nation's top elected officials and the public as well as a key focal point for millions.

Along with the increasing importance of the presidential press secretary, so, too, have we seen a proliferation of people filling the position of organizational spokesperson. This number has increased to the point where it is uncommon today to find an organization—public or private—that does not have a person who fills that role in some capacity (Goodman, 1998). According to the United States Bureau of Labor Statistics, it is projected that the number of public relations specialists will grow by 22.5% by 2020 (author unknown, 2012). While this statistic speaks to the overall number of professional communicators, it can be surmised that organizational spokesmen or press secretaries will be part of that anticipated escalation. This communicator and others who are part of the communication function make them the cohesive entities they are. Communication constitutes organizations (McPhee & Tompkins, 1986). Furthermore, on a broad scale, this speaks to an ever-growing recognition and acceptance of the reality of how vital it is for entities to be able to connect and successfully communicate with their publics. Rare is the day when organizations reap advantages by operating completely under the radar screen of either the general public or their targeted connections. Because of this, a voice is needed to acknowledge and be acknowledged by those external forces. However, there is another layer to this reality. This pertains to an organization's desire or perceived need to control what and how it does communicate to and with its publics.

It is the organization's spokesperson who plays a key role here. In a visible and consistent manner, it is often this professional who serves as the entity's primary intermediary between it and other entities, including the media and general public. How well this person does impacts the success or effectiveness of an organization's ability to connect with its neighbors and community both directly and through the media (Crabtree, 2011). This person's performance also impacts the organization's reputation or image. Furthermore, this professional often is a lead strategist within his or her organization when it comes to devising plans that help position it in a way that is most favorable and conducive to its ongoing efforts to earn profits and maintain a positive reputation. Such strategies include determining when information is shared with the public, by whom, and in what format. At times, it is the organizational spokesman himself or herself who dispenses with the information, while other times it is the chief executive officer or another top-level manager. Specifically, this is often dictated by the circumstance and by the recommendation of that primary spokesperson. What is key, however, is not always so much who is doing the speaking but that the message being imparted is consistent (Smith, 2009).

The organizational spokesman actually plays a number of key roles within his or her company or association. Sometimes this person's role is highly visible and sometimes not. Either way, however the organization does communicate with its targeted publics, almost always the fingerprints of the organizational spokesman are found on decisions on how best to carry out this effort. These professionals interact with the chief executive and other top officers throughout the organization in ways that are both formal and informal. In all interactions, their primary objectives are (1) to continue identifying ways to connect the dots between what and how they represent their employer and client and their appropriate publics and (2) to determine ways that best present the client in the most advantageous way possible. These objectives are met when the spokesman is able to explore and create various internal organizational formats that help instill a sense of common purpose among the various layers that comprise an entity (Krone, 2005).

Not always is this person called an organizational spokesman. The more common term, as in the case of Jerald terHorst, is press secretary. Other titles range from director of communication and director of media relations to something more important-sounding, such as vice president for corporate relations. Titles are often dictated by the size of an organization and how it is structured. Either way, the person carrying out the duties of an organizational spokesman is a key and oftentimes essential player in any entity's outreach or communication efforts.

Personal Reflections

Thank goodness that in the years I worked as a press secretary, I never faced the dilemma that terHorst did. I like to think that, had I, I would have demonstrated the courage of my convictions as terHorst did. I suspect that the great majority of organizational spokesmen never find themselves at the sort of crossroads that terHorst faced. That same majority, of course, never serves as the voice for the president of the United States, either. But this is not to say that what I call "the rest of us" have not and do not face difficult choices in our own spheres. One media representative I know worked at a university that was awarded a sizeable research grant from the Department of Homeland Security. As part of this grant, the university built a state-of-the-art research lab where it tested animals against deadly chemical agents. This particular media rep happened to be a strong and active animal rights advocate. With the grant, this professional was faced with the distinct possibility of having to defend or at least speak to a practice that she morally opposed. What to do? She spoke with her supervisor about her attitude toward animal testing. Fortunately, she did not need or have to resign, as the supervisor agreed to assign other members of the media team to this case.

In another instance, a spokesperson for a county police department learned of several sizeable budget expenditures by her superiors that she believed to be wasteful and unnecessary. She told me of her concern about having to defend them to reporters when she herself believed them to be unjustified. As it turned out, in her dealings with the press, no reporters asked her directly about these budget items. She felt a great deal of relief, as she was not sure if she would have been dispassionate enough to speak to them in a manner that did not reveal her true feelings.

In both examples, I purposefully presented the case studies in vague enough terms as to not reveal the identities of each of the communicators. They told me of their situations in confidence. Nevertheless, the two speak to a reality of life as a spokesman that is not always clear-cut or without some degree of internal struggle. Learning facts and deciding how best to articulate various messages in front of a room of people who are recording, filming, or writing down everything you say is not a small challenge. Exuding public support on behalf of something you question or oppose greatly compounds the matter. To that I say, welcome to the world of organizational spokesmanship!

I have worked professionally in communication for more than four decades. At the beginning of that time, I was one of the reporters tossing out questions—some easy, some not; some thoughtful, some not—to the person facing me and my notepad. My role was one of detachment in the sense that I strove to record what I was told by others. My personal opinion or judgment was of no consequence. Instead, I was charged with being accurate, fair, and coherent in my presentation of the comments given me and the information I was able to collect. (Make no mistake, it is not my intent here to minimize the gravity of what some may consider to be simple charges. Reporters—good ones—perform a vital service to our free society. As a journalism major, my hat forever goes off to them.) As a reporter, however, I did not stand in the spotlight and have to remain professional in demeanor in my response to inquiries or challenges to my words and messages. I did not have to worry about how my words would ultimately be presented by people who owed no allegiance to me or my client. Would my comments, even if reported accurately, be presented out of context? How would my comments be juxtaposed with comments from other people quoted in the same story who had a different or possibly opposing perspective or, at the least, no interest in being in harmony with anything I might be saying? If this did happen, what would be the reaction of my superiors or clients? Would they understand? Would they blame me? As a reporter, these questions were ones of little concern to me. As a press representative, as I came to appreciate, they were certainly on the mind of the person whose words I was representing. Again, welcome to the world of organizational spokesmanship!

The great bulk of my years in communication have been in the role of spokesman. Consequently, those above-listed internal musings were among my most constant companions. Without question, there were times when their collective weight was quite heavy. Fortunately, through years of trial and tribulation, I was able to perceive those trying times in what I deemed a realistic perspective, thus keeping the butterflies in my stomach at bay. These butterflies or nervous flutters were born out of my own innate nervousness. However, at times I did lack confidence in the abilities of some reporters as well as the support from those in my own organization. In my years, I worked for a number of bosses. Some, in my view, were good, and some were not. Some were supportive of me in my spokesman role, while others were not. I was blessed with having some bosses who went out of their way to keep me in the loop of key decisions being made by the top executives. This was a boon to my ability to do my job well. I have also known what it is like to be kept in the dark and be put in a position of having to speak publicly about decisions that I was not as versed in as I would have preferred. Being on both sides of this coin has given me a rounded perspective on the circumstances under which a spokesman should operate. Still, as I never worked for the president of the United States, my interactions with the press, though important, did not carry with them the potential ramifications of terHorst and his peers. Experience also provided me with appreciation of the inner workings of this position and the contribution it makes in that most fundamental action in which we all partake: communication. Also, as a former journalist, I never viewed the press as "the enemy." Rather, to this day I continue seeing them as fellow communicators in a quest to enlighten the general public. Still, coupled with extensive research of the field itself, I have developed not only a deep respect for what the person in front of the microphone or notepad does or attempts to do but also a stronger belief in the need for greater training to be provided to those future communicators with designs on doing spokesmanship for a living. They, too, are communicators, just as much as are other public relations practitioners, journalists, and even me.

The Purpose of This Text

The primary purpose of this text is to provide students of communication, particularly those who have ambitions of eventually pursuing a career as press secretary or spokesperson, with information into both the mechanics of carrying out the duties of such a role, as well as insight into how this function melds within the flow of an organization and its numerous component parts. Such a text that focuses exclusively on the role, challenges, responsibilities, and even history of organizational spokesmanship has not been written until now. There are public relations texts that have devoted portions to this function, but none in which the entire volume is devoted exclusively to spokesmanship. My goal is to provide understanding of what is becoming an increasingly significant role in our society and in the communication profession. I also hope to inspire other scholars to begin pursuing greater analysis of this key function. At present, my research indicates that not only does a text on organizational spokesmanship not exist; neither is any formal credit class on this topic being offered at any university or college. On both counts, change is overdue. One only has to peruse any newspaper on any given day to see numerous articles fueled by comments being given or elicited by spokesmen and women. The same holds true for the electronic media. Furthermore, the media has become or allowed itself to become more dependent on spokesmen than ever before. The result is that not only is the role of spokesmen seen as being of high importance; it has evolved into one of high necessity in both the public and private sectors.

Generally, what coverage the topic of spokesman spokesmanship has been given in professional communication journals pertains more to profiles on prominent people holding down such highly visible jobs as presidential press secretary, critiques of the information flow from an organization to the public in times of a crisis, or analysis of the role of communication in regard to a range of issues, such as internal relations and risk preparation. Though interesting and somewhat helpful, none provide direct analysis into the purpose of such a function or specific insight into the steps one needs to take to eventually attain such a role. While I will not pretend to provide the definitive answer to those points, with this text it is my intent to give this key communication role the analysis it deserves. In our time of mass communication, the one role designed to faithfully represent and speak out on behalf of others warrants a close look-see. Filling this role is often as challenging as the function itself. In addition, the impact of how well a person does in that capacity—positive and negative—can be quite significant and long-lasting. Thus, its importance also dictates the attention of such a text as this.

This text, then, will delve into this position from a range of perspectives. Information and insights that follow will be drawn from research on aspects relating to the topic that has been conducted thus far, my own personal experiences as a former organizational spokesman, and insights from well-respected professionals currently serving in this capacity. Collectively, these topics will provide the reader with a much deeper and broader understanding and (hopefully) appreciation of the role and challenges of this position. Also, this text should discourage any communication students from taking the position of organizational spokesman lightly, for no other reason than the fact that the thousands of entities that have created and filled such a role do not take it lightly. More than that, the role has come to fill a vital need in a culture that looks to and, in many instances, demands an ongoing connectivity between the many entities and individuals who provide services and necessities and the people who seek and/or require them. It is this skilled individual who helps provide and maintain that linkage usually in a very visible way.

This text is divided into chapters, each of which focuses on specific aspects of the organizational spokesman function. A highlight of each chapter is an exclusive interview with a professional who currently works as an organizational spokesman. I hand-picked these professionals based on their outstanding reputations as professional communicators and their willingness to share some wisdom with others, and because, collectively, they represent a range of fields in both the private and public sectors. Highlights of the interviews are published here. Each interview focuses primarily on the thrust of the chapter in which it is featured. In addition, each chapter concludes with a list of chapter highlights and several discussion questions designed to generate further examination of the overall topic. Following is a brief chapter-by-chapter snapshot of the questions and topics that will be explored within each chapter.

Chapter 1: General Overview

What is an organizational spokesman? Is this person little more than a mouthpiece for an entity? Is this a professional who is told what to say, and, then, much like a child's doll, a string is pulled from his or her back and the person simply continues to repeat whatever words or message he or she has been programmed to say? These questions will be explored from various perspectives, including taking a look at the job and determining both what an organizational spokesman is and is not. Addressing these fundamental questions will provide the reader with a clear understanding of the workings of this unique professional communicator. Also, from a broad perspective, the various roles such a professional plays in the context of an organization's day-to-day activities as well as in a range of various scenarios will be explored.

Another fundamental question will be examining why such a communicator is needed in the first place. What impact, if any, would there be if the function of spokesman was eliminated? What difference would this make to an organization's top officers, to the organization's workers or members, or to the public it attempts to serve and/or connect with? Addressing these questions will be tied to an overview of the history of the function itself. How long has it existed? How did it come to be? After all, everything has a beginning, and the position of organizational spokesman is no exception. What has been the evolution of the role this professional plays? Has it changed much, if at all, over the years?

Finally, as the function of organizational spokesman falls under the general umbrella of public relations, what is the difference between the two? Specifically, how do the responsibilities, functions, and goals of a spokesman compare with those of the person who serves as an organization's public relations director? For instance, how concerned is the spokesman with generating publicity for his or her organization? Furthermore, is there any difference between ways in which each measures the success or effectiveness of his or her efforts?

Chapter 2: Organizational Role

In an exploration of the role of an organizational spokesman, this chapter delves in greater specifics into the question of how this professional fits in with his or her colleagues. Does such a professional maintain a role defined more by its consistency, or does that role change depending on the situation at hand? In other words, is an organizational spokesman like a chameleon in that his or her priorities change depending on the circumstances or surroundings?

Traditionally, an organizational spokesman is considered to be more of an external communicator—the entity's ultimate representative. Should this be the case? If so, what is the dynamic between the spokesman and the media and/or the general public? Is there a mutual dependency between them (Theus, 1993)? If so, how, then, does it fit in with an organization's internal structure? Does the person who fills this role have any meaningful connection or reason to be interested in and knowledgeable of his or her coworkers or internal issues that might be of concern to him or her?

In keeping with these questions and the matter of this communicator's exact role, the following duties and responsibilities of the spokesman will be examined: efforts to help devise messaging strategies for the organization and its key members, risk and crisis communication, working with the media, external relations beyond the media, and internal relations.

Chapter 3: Measuring Success and Effectiveness

How does an organizational spokesman know whether he or she has done a good job? What exactly are this person's goals? Does the spokesman, in fact, have any exact goals, other than to speak well on behalf of the client or organization without making any misstatements or mistakes? If the responsibilities of the position are more complex than that, what are they? Are the goals of the spokesman tied to those of the organization, more to the person's own individual performance, or both (Thompson & McEwen, 1958)? An example of one responsibility might be to help the organization accurately adapt to its environment, especially as the environment changes (Organ, 2004). Furthermore, what are the pitfalls or communication barriers that serve as potential impediments to a spokesman's job being well done? Beyond that, what are ways to overcome or contend with those barriers?

In keeping with this particular focus, what are the dos and don'ts when it comes to being an organizational spokesman? For instance, is there a dress code? Is there a certain way of behaving when interacting with reporters and members of the media? What should the spokesman's relationship be with other communicators within the same organization? How closely should they collaborate? These and other fundamental questions will be examined in this chapter.

Chapter 4: Legal and Ethical Aspects

How free from legal responsibility or accountability is the spokesman? Is he or she free to stand in front of a group of reporters and say whatever he or she wants about another organization, person, or product, for instance? If others dispute or protest against what the spokesman has said or been quoted as saying, is it an adequate defense from the spokesman to claim that he or she was simply saying what he or she were told or hired to say? Can those who feel they have been wronged sue a spokesman?

Beyond the legality of what a spokesman can and cannot do, what is this person's degree of vulnerability to the organization itself? What happens, for example, when the spokesman is misquoted or his or her comments are misrepresented by the press? What challenges, if any, does this create for the spokesman, not just with the media but with the members of the organization itself? What is the impact on the spokesman's reputation in the eyes of those with whom he or she works and to whom he or she reports? If mistakes with the media and public occur, what steps can the spokesman take to help address the matter with his or her peers? Such questions speak to the core of a spokesman's various internal and external relationships. In the context of the spokesman's legal and ethical considerations, what steps should this communicator take to help ensure his or her links to others remain strong and positive?

Chapter 5: The Road to Spokesmanship

What is the path to becoming an organizational spokesman? How does one go from graduating from college, for example, to being able to stand in front of a room full of reporters, answering their questions or providing to them information that comes from a range of talking points? What are the doors that one must go through to get from diploma to microphone? What skills or qualities should one possess? Presently, a clear road map does not exist. However, enough benchmarks are present to assist those looking to pursue such a job. As such a straightforward career path has yet to be established, analysis from a broad perspective of these benchmarks dominates this chapter. Complementing this list will be a breakdown of the skill set, along with particular personality characteristics a person should have and appreciate to help in his or her journey.

Chapter 6: The Future

It is always a bit dangerous to gaze into the future and outline what lies ahead, particularly when no one has traveled that path before you. Still, there are more than enough indicators to assess the future of the organizational spokesman in terms of such areas as job growth, the spokesman's role in the working world and even in our personal lives, and the challenges facing those who find themselves either by choice or circumstance serving as the official spokesperson for others.

Chapter One

General Overview

What is an organizational spokesman, anyway? The answer to that question has multiple layers. The spokesperson, for starters, is the person who provides the public, including the media, with information. This comes either in the form of a public statement, the sharing of talking points, or responding to questions from the media. The spokesman for an organization is not or does not have to be the same person all the time. As we will discuss, the person in front of the microphone might vary depending on a particular circumstance. Sometimes it is the designated press secretary, while at other times it is another administrator or even the organization's chief executive. Who is given the honor of taking questions from reporters or speaking on behalf of the organization is usually part of the entity's strategy for handling a situation at any given time. Normally, however, the organizational spokesman is one specific person serving as the primary "voice" and "face" for his or her entity. In fact, in the mind of the public, it is not uncommon for this person to become synonymous with the organization he or she represents. This is why it is vital that such a person be articulate, credible, and personable. In addition, this person needs to be serious, yet have a good "bedside manner."

Is such a person the same for all groups, or does the role of this professional vary from entity to entity? Is a president's press secretary, for instance, the same as a spokesman for a local board of education? Usually, but not always. But in exploring these fundamental questions, a good place to start is by placing "organizational spokesman" in the context of the broader concept of public relations itself. After all, it is the social science of public relations from which all elements of professional communication derive. As the term suggests, "public relations" speaks to the efforts of one entity to link or connect with another. The entities can range from an individual to an organization to a singular public or multiple publics. The actual connection made can and often does vary in length in that it can be very brief or have a long shelf life. For instance, you see a spot on television advertising the opening of a new movie. The next night you go see it because the advertising spot made the movie seem appealing. That is one form of public relations. Another is when several organizations, such as multiple neighborhood associations, join forces to speak out against an issue in which they are both concerned. The example involving the new movie speaks to public relations geared to persuade. The other example speaks to public relations designed to establish and maintain an alliance or partnership.

The concepts of persuasion and partnership were first articulated by Grunig and Hunt (1984) in their introduction of four models of public relations. They called the first two *press agentry* and *public information.* The press agentry model spoke to an anything-goes style of public relations, in which truth and accuracy are not major factors when it comes to generating visibility for a product or client. The public information model pertained to a style in which the communicator focused entirely on presenting information to the public in an objective, straightforward manner, without any attempt to shade, slant, or manipulate it. It was the second of the two models, however, that presented public relations as an effort either to persuade or to establish alliances or partnerships. These models, respectfully, were called two-way asymmetrical and two-way symmetrical. A discussion of each is necessary, as they speak to the dual goals of a spokesman when he or she represents a client or organization.

Elements of the two-way asymmetrical model were introduced during World War I by the Creel Committee, a group organized by President Woodrow Wilson to promote the purchase of war bonds. In its work, the committee, headed by George Creel, tapped into the psychological principle of mass persuasion. They did this by purposefully constructing messages that appealed to what people wanted to hear and believe. In their messaging, the committee successfully triggered emotional responses from the American public (MacDougall, 1952) by capitalizing on the patriotic feelings many were feeling at that time. One of the members of this committee was Edward Bernays, who became one of the pioneers of the public relations movement. Bernays's career and numerous campaigns revolved around the notion of utilizing public relations to persuade and emotionally manipulate the public or aspects of it. Other practitioners followed in his footsteps. One notable disciple was John Hill, cofounder of the still very successful public relations firm of Hill & Knowlton. In describing the two-way asymmetrical model that Bernays introduced and that Hill followed, Hill said that he sought to win over public opinion through the interpretation of facts and the power of persuasion (Hill, 1963).

Regarding the two-way symmetrical model, it was scholars Scott Cutlip and Allen Center (1952) who first viewed public relations as the practice of attempting to bring two publics into harmonious adjustment by communicating and interpreting information, ideas, and opinions. Generally, this occurs or is attempted when several publics share an interest in or a concern for a particular issue. An easy example would be two groups that support the same political candidate. They join forces to work on that person's behalf. This, coupled with the two-way asymmetrical model, touches on the essence of a spokesman's effort: to generate support and maintain positive ties.

Over the years, literally hundreds of formal definitions of public relations have been put forth. Textbooks have been written about public relations. College degree programs have been built around the field. In addition, throughout much of the 20th century, a great many communication theories and models were introduced, all attempting to explain and analyze the workings of the fundamental act of people reaching out to each other. Sometimes the "reaching out" is one-way—as in the example of the new movie—and other times it is more two-way—as in the example of the two neighborhood associations. Communication, of course, comes in many forms and through many channels: verbal, nonverbal, written, oral, via social media, via advertising, by giving a speech, via telephone, by writing a letter, via carrier pigeon (by the way, does anybody use carrier pigeon anymore?), through face-to-face meetings, and so on. As it involves people, communication or public relations can be quite complex at times. At other times it can be direct and simple.

One reason the act of communicating by organizations or other formal structures is often viewed as being complex and multilayered is that so many people have their own perception or perspective as to what it is. For instance, one only has to visit a number of organizations or companies to discover differences in the title and duties of each entity's communication officer. This is very common. The range of titles, duties, and job descriptions can be such things as director of public relations, director of media relations, and even director of marketing. A major factor in the specific title a communication officer is given is often dictated by the concept of public relations the chief executive officer has. He or she, for example, may see this person's main role as writing speeches because this is what the organization's chief need is. Another may see the communication function as being simply to generate positive publicity for the organization, as he or she believes that greater visibility is what the organization or business requires most. Still, another may see the communication officer's main duty as handling all advertising. No matter the title and specific duties, each of the men and women holding down these positions are involved in some form of reaching out and attempting to make a durable connection with others.

Generally, the larger in size and payroll an organization is, the more communication officers they are likely to employ. At the same time, the greater number of communication officers within an organization, then the more likely each person is apt to be responsible for a specific aspect of information sharing. One person may handle the organization's internal newsletter, for instance, while another may focus exclusively on writing and distributing press releases or announcements. And then there is the organizational spokesman. Collectively, these roles and their duties speak to the complexity of the public relations function itself.

This takes us back to the focus of this text: the organization's spokesman. This professional and position fall under the broad umbrella of public relations. The spokesman, for many entities, has evolved into becoming a key tool in an organization's effort to maintain a level of visibility, respectability, aura of openness, and connectivity with others. We see this in politics, in the corporate world, in areas of community service, in higher education, in the entertainment field, and even in the efforts of individuals seeking to gain notoriety or some degree of sustained visibility. The organizational spokesman is a well-established niche that has evolved into becoming as commonplace in its existence as it is greatly utilized. Thus, in the context of public relations, this role or function is viewed as one primary public relations tool for those entities wishing to reach out to external audiences.

Earlier, I alluded to the fact that hundreds of definitions of public relations have been put forth over the years by practitioners and scholars. Though with much merit, none could be found that directly mentions the duties or efforts of a spokesman. However, one has recently been created that is worth noting. It is germane to our topic, even though it, too, does not specifically mention *organizational spokesman*. The difference here is that it alludes to it.

New Definition of Public Relations

The Public Relations Society of America (PRSA) announced what it terms a modern definition of public relations that is in keeping with a new era of the communication profession. This is noteworthy, as it serves as a benchmark for how this organization, the largest of its kind in the world, now defines public relations. It also sets the tone under which practitioners are encouraged to carry out their assignments and engage and interact with others. PRSA now defines *public relations* as "a strategic communication process that builds mutually beneficial relationships between organizations and their publics" (PRSA, 2012). This definition was the result of much debate and input from a wide range of scholars and professional practitioners. In the end, PRSA conducted a national poll in which more than 1,000 PRSA members voted. The result was this new definition. One of its highlights is that it acknowledges the importance of cooperation and collaboration between entities. How the organizational spokesman fits into this dynamic serves as a key parameter by which his or her role is characterized in relation to the overall organization and its members and to the appropriate members of the general public. Is the spokesman a mere advocate or a key bridge builder? Taking this question one step further, is it possible for the spokesman to be both? This is a fundamental question we will be delving into in greater depth throughout this text.

While this recently set definition of public relations by PRSA should not be ignored or downplayed, nor should other, earlier depictions of this social science. They have contributed to how public relations as a field of study and practice is perceived and, in many ways, practiced. Through the years, hundreds of definitions of public relations have been set forth. One of the first was set forth by Bernays, considered by many to be the father of public relations, in part, because he was the first to actually teach a college-level course on this topic. Bernays (1923) initially viewed public relations as a management function designed to secure public understanding and acceptance of an organization's policies and interests. On the surface, this seems to coincide nicely with PRSA's most recent definition. Bernays, however, was a strong proponent of public manipulation via such strategies as creative media events and corralling public opinion to support a particular cause or product. Thus, in the case of Bernays, harmony was sought by motivating one or more publics to change their attitude or take action they might not undertake without the spokesman's well-planned efforts. The PRSA definition speaks more to partnership—a dynamic to which the spokesman seems well suited.

Another definition, this one articulated by another practitioner, is that *public relations* is the act of "doing good and making sure you get caught" (Seifert, 1984, p. 7). This definition, while clever enough, also speaks to the concept that public relations speaks to self-promotion, that is, devising strategies to communicate positive information, perspectives, and so forth about one's self. It is not all that different from the definition articulated by Bernays more than 60 years prior. Both suggest well-planned efforts to promote a particular side, person, product, and so on. In this context, one can easily perceive the role of organizational spokesman as being the man or woman who is the primary advocate of such a one-sided stance. It is this person who regularly provides the media and other publics with favorable or self-serving information and then addresses any questions or contrary perspectives that might be stated in response to the initial statements.

Thus, in the context of this kind of public relations advocacy, the organizational spokesman is a principal player. One might even say it is the purpose of this professional to serve as a faithful advocate for the organization or client (Goodman, 1998). However, though effective, it should be noted that public relations advocacy does have its limits (Kruckeberg & Starck, 2000). After all, life being what it is, not all promotional efforts are 100% successful. (Not everyone drinks Coca Cola, for example. Some people actually prefer Pepsi or other soft drinks.) Given this reality, public relations as more of a relationship-building exercise has evolved into becoming a more popular and well-regarded form of outreach, particularly on a long-term basis (Kruckeberg, Starck, & Vujnovic, 2006). This is because making an effort to insert an organization into its surrounding community better serves society as well as the organization itself. Practically speaking, an organization is successful only if it is within the context and general acceptance of society. A relationship management model, as introduced by Ledingham and Bruning (2000a), speaks to this. It is in the context of public relations that go beyond the immediate needs of an organization that the role of organizational spokesman becomes a bit more complex and nuanced. Here, the organizational spokesman does more than simply tout the strengths and attributes of his or her client. Instead, the spokesman does so in relationship to the organization's surrounding environment. How well does the organization blend with its environment? Is the organization a metaphorical island within its region or community, or is it a logical part of the landscape? In other words, the spokesman's message must speak both to his or her organization's individual merits as well as the fact that it is a good neighbor and community member. In addition, the spokesman should communicate in a manner that helps foster positive ties with the public. While people do not begrudge the reality that a company strives to make money, they do tend to feel greater empathy toward organizations and companies that are also working on behalf of the greater good of society. As society itself is the ultimate stakeholder for any organization (Starck & Kruckeberg, 2001), it is essential that it feels some degree of comfort with the organization's existence and stated purpose. The spokesman can help ensure that his or her organization maintains positive ties with its surrounding community.

Big Picture Versus Immediate Picture

This, then, points to the dual challenge of the organizational spokesman: presenting the entity's broad, big-picture purpose as well as its more exact, immediate goals—big picture and immediate picture. The two are not mutually exclusive, nor should they be presented in a way that suggests that. At the same time, doing so is not always easy, as their commonality may not seem apparent at times. In fact, there may even be circumstances where the two conflict. An example may be found on days of inclement weather when school systems are forced to decide whether to cancel classes for the day. The big picture goal of any school system is to provide its students with an education of high quality. But when a heavy snow falls, how does an organizational spokesman explain that overarching commitment when roads are icy, travel to and from school is a bit treacherous, and the odds of forgoing that opportunity for education are quite strong? How does the spokesman reconcile the two?

The challenge is real because not everyone will agree with a decision to close school for a day or even a few hours. But even if they do, it is still the spokesman's job to remind all concerned that inclement weather does not alter the school system's overriding commitment to the education of the children. For me, when faced with such a challenge in my time as a press secretary for a university, I made it a point to remind reporters and the general public that the safety and physical well-being of the children was linked to their ability to receive an education. Even if a point such as this seems obvious, such a scenario as inclement weather remains an opportunity to remind any and all who are listening of the institution's bottom-line purpose.

Another real-world example is found when an organization hires a new chief executive officer. Obviously, this is an important moment for the organization. But for the spokesman, it also represents a challenge to properly combine the big picture–immediate picture elements of that person's job. On the one hand, there is the challenge of sharing information about the new CEO in a way that properly presents his or her biography and why that person was selected for the job. On the other hand, this person must be introduced in a way that links his or her background with the vision of the organization. If done well, the spokesman is able to help reassure the organization's publics and stakeholders that a sound decision has been made, so the entity will continue to move forward in a smooth and positive way, even with a new CEO who brings with him or her a new leadership style. There are also times, of course, when this is not always easy, such as when a person with a controversial background has been hired.

Spokesman Versus Media Relations Officer

The simple, earlier example of a possible school cancellation because of inclement weather serves as a good lead-in to the primary differences in duties between an organizational spokesman and the entity's media or public relations officer. The first obvious difference is organizational spokesmen are more visible. They are the ones in front of a camera or standing before print reporters and sharing information, explaining positions taken by the organization, and usually ending up being quoted by the press. In the case of an inclement weather announcement, it is the spokesman serving as the primary point of contact to both the media and general public regarding such a widespread announcement. At those times, should members of the public, including the press, have questions, it is the spokesman or his or her office to which they turn to get answers.

The media or public relations officer is far more behind the scenes. This professional normally devotes his or her expertise and energies to getting reporters to cover stories about various aspects of the organization, including some of its people, such as the chief executive officer, when it is appropriate. He or she arranges interviews and tries to promote coverage of the organization to help facilitate a positive perception of it as well as enhance its image. But this person's work is less out front. Ideally, while such a communication professional and the organization's spokesman should keep each other well informed of what they are doing, each has his or her own specific area of responsibility.

A second, major difference pertains to the matter alluded to earlier: big picture versus immediate picture. No one would disagree that an organization's chief executive officer needs to maintain a keen awareness of all issues facing every aspect of the business, company, or association. For this person to be effective, his or her level of knowledge about what it is he or she oversees must be as wide as it is deep. Furthermore, to maintain such a level of knowledge, he or she should have a strong enough tie with major players throughout the organization in order to raise questions with them, engage in discussion of matters of concern as well as things that are going well, and have a general sense of the strengths, weaknesses, and challenges facing the range of units and/or departments. The other administrator who should possess the same degree of knowledge and have the same breadth of contacts is the organizational spokesman.

On any given day, at any given moment, the spokesman may be called on to provide to the media and general public up-to-date information about any unit within the organization. If something goes wrong unexpectedly in the organization's physical plant, for instance, the spokesman needs to have a vital enough base of knowledge of that unit or office to help it better understand its workings and, if necessary, articulate to reporters the specifics of the situation. Sometimes predicaments arise that are unforeseen, yet are dramatic enough to draw immediate attention from outside groups. The immediacy of the occurrence may make it difficult, if not impossible, for the spokesman to be thoroughly or properly educated about the unit affected. But already having a sound base of knowledge helps keep the spokesman in an appropriate state-of-readiness for the unexpected.

One good example of this is one that is also highly dramatic: the attack on the World Trade Center in New York City on September 11, 2001. In this case, even though the primary spokesman turned out to be the city's CEO, mayor Rudy Giuliani, the principle of maintaining a high level of knowledge about each of the major units within an entity remained. In his book on leadership (2002), Giuliani described preparedness as being a vital key to effective leadership, particularly in times of the unexpected. His knowledge, in this case, of the city's emergency operations and the people in charge of them enabled Giuliani to carry out his duties as the "voice" of the city as well as he did. This meant that during nonemergency times, Giuliani needed to maintain an open line of communication on a regular basis with each of New York City's units.

The question, then, for the spokesman is, how can one best maintain such a constant state of readiness? How can one best maintain an adequate level of knowledge about the entire organization? This is one of the main points of discussion in the next chapter. However, for the purposes here, this is one reason why it is essential for the organization's spokesman to have close ties with the CEO and for his or her boss to allow him or her the freedom or latitude to connect and work with others on a regular basis. The spokesman, in many ways, must be as visible to an organization's internal base as he or she is to its external publics. He or she must also develop a mind-set that matches that of the organization's top officer. More than most, l, the spokesman represents the chief officer as well as the organization itself. This is because in the mind of much of the public, it is the chief officer who is the one person above all who most represents the organization, no matter how visible he or she might be. The organization's spokesman, then, is that person's surrogate, particularly in matters of speaking on behalf of the entity.

Why Is an Organizational Spokesman Needed?

Why, one might ask, does the CEO need a surrogate? Would the main boss suddenly be rendered ineffective if his or her organization did not have an official spokesman? Aren't CEOs supposed to be articulate and competent enough to speak in front of a room full of reporters or members of the general public? Indeed, would the organization itself fail to make money or properly provide services to the public if it did not have any one in that role or, for that matter, such a position within its internal structure? Perhaps a bit surprisingly, the answer to each of those questions is not necessarily or automatically no. Sure, life would certainly continue for the CEO and the organization if it did not have a spokesman. But the question is, would that life be better? Would the work of the CEO be any less stressful if he or she did not have a spokesman serving as both a buffer to and liaison with the general public and/or media? Let's take these and related questions one at a time.

Without question, any chief executive officer recognizes and values effective communication. In the words of author and scholar Charles Barnard, "The first executive function is to develop and maintain a system of communication" (1938, p. 226). In executives' capacity as leaders, these men and women know that for their vision and efforts to be successful, they must be communicated to their designated publics in ways that are timely and well-understood and reinforce a positive image of their company or organization. On top of that, the top executive and his or her managers are constantly on the receiving end of an array of communiqués (Lorch, 1978). Given that, they know the importance of ensuring people of competence are given the responsibility of helping facilitate all communicate efforts. One such function in the overall communication effort is the role of serving as the organization's public representative. This role of a spokesman is to speak on behalf of the client or organization. These professionals do this by disseminating information or by being an advocate for that which they represent—even if the organization's policies and positions run counter to their personal perspectives. Without question, the CEO is capable of doing this, too. But the CEO does not always have the time to give daily or regular briefings. The spokesman does.

Also, there is the fact that the CEO may not always be the best person to speak on behalf of the company or organization. The organization may want to speak with one voice, of course, but that does not necessarily mean one specific person will be doing the speaking (Smith, 2009). Who does the speaking or representing depends on the situation. In fact, depending on the situation, others within the organization may be more appropriate than either the CEO or the traditional spokesperson. We will delve into this in greater detail in Chapter 2.

Communication is central to almost everything an organization and its staff members and administrators do (Stillman, 2005). In addition, depending on the merit of its execution, communication also keeps each of the units within an organization in sync and the overall entity closely tied to its external publics, including clients, customers, and stakeholders. Is there one individual or office that is in the best position to help ensure this happens? Not necessarily. As mentioned earlier, the answer to that may depend on the specific situation at hand. If a university closes for a day because of an outbreak of campus violence, initially the chief of police rather than the traditional spokesman may be the best person representing the institution. Later on, when things have settled down, the spokesman may return to the podium or microphone.

In the eyes of the general public, often it is the chief officer or president of an organization who is the one person more than any other equated with that entity. Obviously we do this with the president of the United States when we think of the federal government. The same is generally true when it comes to universities, major corporations, and service organizations, to name a few examples. These executives are in charge, and, ultimately, it is the decisions they make that determine the success or nonsuccess of what they oversee. From a communication perspective, then, the chief executive is the organization's chief symbol. As part of this, how the general public and the organization's stakeholders perceive that man or woman coincides with how they perceive both the organization itself and the product or service it provides. As the executive and his or her organization are joined at the hip, it is important for that organization's public relations and marketing apparatus to ensure the chief officer's image remains as positive as the organization's.

Case Studies

This takes us back to the previous point that sometimes it is not always appropriate for the chief officer to be the one serving as the entity's spokesman. Generally, it is best for the leader and the organization to be showcased only at those times that are most favorable to him or her. This helps the executive maintain a positive public persona, thus helping safeguard how the organization itself is perceived. Unfortunately, there are times when someone needs to represent the organization when things are not quite so sunny. In fact, a situation may arise when the person speaking on behalf of the organization may have to emit negative information or speak to an occurrence that is sensitive and/or controversial. This is an appropriate time for a person other than the chief officer to be in the spotlight. The obvious person is the organizational spokesman, but sometimes even that is not always the best way to go. Following are two examples that illustrate this point with both a positive and negative perspective. One is an episode where the chief officer should have served as the organization's primary spokesman but did not, and the other is one in which the chief executive was right not to be out front.

- In May 1985, a confrontation between Philadelphia police and a black activist cult called MOVE resulted in the downfall of the city's then-mayor, W. Wilson Goode (Nabel, 1991). Prior to this event, Goode was widely perceived as being an effective, highly competent city mayor. City police were involved in an armed conflict with this group, which was lodged in a fortified row house. Police dropped plastic explosives onto the roof of the row house where MOVE members were barricaded. Unfortunately and unexpectedly, the explosives triggered a fire, which ended up burning out of control, destroying more than 60 homes and leaving nearly 250 people homeless. Until then, much of Goode's popularity was based on the perception that he was viewed as being an active and hands-on administrator. But when the MOVE incident occurred, Goode suddenly seemed anything but engaged. According to a report by the Philadelphia Special Investigation Commission, Goode followed the advice of staff members who recommended that he distance himself from the situation's command post (author unknown, 1986). Doing so compromised the communication structure. The communication breakdown and the mayor's perceived disengagement from the incident contributed to the heavy criticism he received in the aftermath of the failed operation.
- In fall 2002, the Washington, D.C., region and surrounding Maryland and Virginia suburbs were caught in the grip of what came to be called the D.C. sniper incident (Censer, 2010). This was a series of seemingly random killings in which five people were killed by unknown assailants over a 21-day period. As a result of heavy media coverage, adults and children found themselves caught in the drama of this unique situation. Not surprisingly, as the tragedy unfolded, they hungered for information as one way of being able to cope with the danger before them. The person who emerged as the primary spokesman during this time was not the major or county executive of any of the jurisdictions or even any of the governors of the affected states. Instead, it was Montgomery County police chief Charles Moose. While Moose was not the only person who provided the media and public with updates, he emerged as the one most connected with speaking on behalf of the authorities responsible for apprehending the snipers.

  This was not a positive event. It was one of great concern to members of the public in that the longer it went on, the more feelings of fear and worry surfaced in them. Thus, what they needed most was information and even reassurance from a figure with perceived expertise in the field of law enforcement. This is why Chief Moose, as opposed to his superior, such as a county executive or other elected official, was a better for the job of spokesman in this matter.

In each incident, public perception was fueled by how well the communication aspect was handled. In Philadelphia, the public was upset because things went so off-track and because they felt the mayor was disengaged and, as a result, failed to provide them with an adequate explanation of why things happened the way they did. In the sniper incident, Moose and the police satisfied the public's need to know in terms of the content of their information and the frequency with which it was shared. Communication did not lessen the gravity of either situation. But in the case of Philadelphia, the fact that it was handled poorly enhanced the public's negative reaction. In the second incident, a successful communication effort helped the public cope with the terror and uncertainty of it.

Cyrano de Bergerac

"My greatest victories were won under an assumed name." This is a quote spoken by the title character in *Cyrano de Bergerac*, a drama penned in 1897 by the French playwright Edmond Rostand. In this famous play, because of what he considers to be his hideous features, the articulate and dashing de Bergerac is too afraid to openly declare his love for the beautiful Roxanne. He then comes upon Christian, a decent enough fellow who is smitten with Roxanne, yet who is clumsy with words and expressing his feelings. de Bergerac devises a scheme to serve as the voice for Christian by providing him with the proper words to woo Roxanne. This scheme allows de Bergerac the opportunity to express his own feelings toward Roxanne and help give his true love a chance to find happiness, even if it is not with him.

Through de Bergerac, Christian tells Roxanne, "Your name is like a golden bell hung in my heart, and when I think of you, I tremble, and the bell swings and rings, 'Roxanne!'"

Who would not want a spokesman of that caliber? Though it was not the author's intent, Rostand depicted the potential power of a spokesman as well as the choice one makes when stepping into the role of communication representative. As artful and articulate as a spokesman might be or become, one should always remember that this person is speaking on behalf of the client, not himself or herself. The purpose of the spokesman's words is to showcase others, including a chief executive officer and the members of the organization that person oversees, not himself or herself. The moment the spokesman begins expressing his or her views on issues rather those of whom they have been hired to represent is the moment the spokesman loses his or her effectiveness in that role. The spokesman's loyalty is to both the client and to the message. In maintaining that loyalty, there are times—not often—that arise when one must speak on behalf of something with which he or she disagrees. At this point, one finds himself or herself at a crossroads. As we learned at the outset of this text, for terHorst, he chose to resign rather than defend or justify his boss's decision. In the case of Rostand's fictitious de Bergerac, the title character chose to totally invest himself into boosting another at his expense.

There are other important lessons to learn from this play as well. As inspiring and moving as *Cyrano de Bergerac* was in many ways, Rostand's classic was also a tragedy on a number of communication levels. To begin, I start with faint praise. The title character was a very effective spokesman. de Bergerac's scheme worked, as Christian came across as being very glib, articulate, and poetic in his encounters with Roxanne. As a result, he got the girl. But that result did not make the so-called success of the scheme any less hollow. After all, it was actually de Bergerac who wanted to win the hand of Roxanne. That never happened. Finally, at the play's conclusion, when Roxanne learned the true author of the magical words and the true love behind them, de Bergerac was dying.

Further, de Bergerac deceived his "public" in the form of Roxanne. She thought it was Christian who was actually so articulate and, as a result, fell in love with him and his words. It was not until the very end of the play when she realized the true source of those heartfelt words and feelings. Organizational spokesmen do not use such deception. Communication is never more effective and truer than when it is carried out openly and without trickery, no matter how pure the motive. The fact that de Bergerac was never revealed as the true author of the loving words spoken by Christian until moments before his death made both him and Roxanne victims of his deception. My point here is not to present a literary analysis of this play, but rather take advantage of its points that are quite relevant to our discussion of the role of organizational spokesman. At the time the play was first performed, this communication role existed, but it was far from prominent.

Evolution of the Spokesman

So, how did the position of organizational spokesman come to be in the first place? Certainly over the past near-half-century, one would be hard-pressed to find examples of when sizable entities from the private and public sectors were not represented by some type of public communicator. Prior to that, examples are far fewer in number, particularly in terms of how it relates to the role and responsibilities of spokesmen in today's world. Looking back over the years, there were, of course, many who voiced opinions to the public via the channels of communication available to them. In the early years of the United States, for instance, many of the men who are now viewed as being among our founding fathers were quite prominent in their outspokenness.

Today, it is not unusual for entities such as government agencies to have one person designated as their spokesman. Generally, this is all this particular professional does and all he or she is known to do by the public. Historically, this was not the case. When people thought of an entity such as a business, agency, or arm of the government, it was the principal leader to which they turned for updates, statements, and so forth. Even if this kind of information was delivered in writing, it was still the leader to whom people turned for information and clarification—even if that chief officer was not a particularly visible person. Business titan John D. Rockefeller was one example. Yes, he interacted with a number of individuals on his staff. But he was not someone who made a habit of appearing in public forums. Citizens did not have multiple sources of information to turn to back then as all of us do today. Thus, their perspective for gaining information was much more narrow. In today's world, thanks in large measure to technology, people are not so dependent on one source of information, including a CEO or commander-in-chief. Not only does the increased technology, largely in the form of the Internet and social media, provide citizens with a greater range of options from which to gain information about a particular business or entity; it provides chief executives with a greater number of options through which to keep any unwanted spotlight off themselves. One primary option is the spokesman. This man or woman is able to go a long way toward filling this void. He or she is able to become the go-to person, in the eyes and ears of the public, who fills the role of the organization's most visible and steady representative.

It is in the area of national politics where the earliest examples of the spokesman are found—specifically, in the executive branch of the federal government. One of the very first spokesman in this realm was a friend and supporter of president Andrew Jackson. His name was Amos Kendall, a newspaper man who served as postmaster general in both the administrations of presidents Jackson and Martin Van Buren. Kendall was viewed by many as being one of the intellectual engines behind Jackson in particular (Cutlip, 1995). Kendall's newspaper experience as a reporter and, later, editor enabled him to be a driving force in interpreting, verbalizing, and even documenting many of Jackson's ideas and wishes (Schlesinger, 1945). Relations between the executive branch and the media then were very different in Kendall's time. As the press was not nearly as proactive or aggressive in their efforts to seek direct comments and face time with top administrators, Kendall and those who followed were more easily able to control information they wished to disseminate to the public (Partington, 2002).

For a public spokesman, Kendall was unique in that he played a vital role in the decisions made by his presidents, both in terms of reaching and communicating with them. Also, the fact he was a visible player in the Jackson and Van Buren administrators was not common for someone in a communication role. Though Kendall, at least among students and scholars of communication, remains a known figure, his notoriety has not been shared by the many who followed him. There of course have been exceptions. Also, this is not to minimize the competence and achievements of those who did following Kendall. Collectively, they did contribute—and continue to do so—to the overall evolution of communication itself and, more specifically, to the rising acceptance of public relations as an essential element in the growth of the numerous entities that comprise society.

In addition to Kendall, another individual who deserves to be mentioned in any historical overview of organizational spokesmanship is Ivy Lee. In fact, Lee, far more than Kendall, had a significant impact on the role of spokesman. Like Kendall, Lee was a former journalist who gained prominence in the field of public relations. His moment came when business tycoon John D. Rockefeller turned to Lee for assistance in a public incident that was damaging Rockefeller's personal and professional reputation. Known to the general public as the Ludlow Massacre, this tragic event occurred in 1915 at the site of the Colorado Fuel and Iron Company camp. Workers employed by Rockefeller went on strike. Violence ensued. Members of the Colorado National Guard and camp guards employed by the Colorado Fuel and Iron Company attacked the workers, killing nearly 25 people, including two women and 11 children (Foner, 1980). The incident received national attention, resulting in outrage against the owner of the fuel and iron company—Rockefeller. Many historians described it was one of the worst atrocities in the history of labor relations (Zinn, 1990).

Rockefeller's son, John D. Junior, turned to Lee for guidance as to what they could do to help quell the negative attention that was being directed toward the Rockefeller name and its numerous holdings. Lee advised Rockefeller Junior to present the family's views fully and frankly—to trust the truth (Chernow, 1998). Rockefeller Junior was so impressed with Lee's guidance that he told a colleague, "Mr. Lee is very much more than a publicity agent. He is one of our advisers in regard to various matters of policy" (Chernow, 1990, p. 584). The recommendations Lee made to Rockefeller were very much in keeping with his philosophy about public relations: present the facts and let the public make their own determinations based on them. Lee's principles revolved around truth, openness, and reality (Hiebert, 1966). Lee believed he could best serve as an advocate for his clients by ensuring their perspectives on any given issue were fully shared with the public, without any kind of shading or calculated omission of information. As admirable or notable as Lee's philosophy may seem, It has not been one that was or is followed by public relations practitioners since. More and more, we see communication efforts driven largely to persuade.

The emergence of Lee and his relationship with the Rockefellers points to a direct link between leadership and communication. Leaders of any note have always been concerned with their image, not so much because of their own personal egos but more because it might impact what they believe or the business they direct. Thus, as was the case with Rockefeller, they maintain an ongoing concern as to how they are being perceived by the general public, which obviously consists of customers and clients (Pimlott, 1951). This speaks to the information the public either has or has access to about any entity and the person or persons in charge of it. What are people thinking about us? Is it accurate? Does it correspond with how we perceive ourselves? How is this affecting our image and quest for greater stability and profit? These and other similar questions—all understandable and legitimate—are ones that leaders have been wrestling with for years, not just in today's world. Going back even before the time of Kendall, American businessmen have been solicitous of public approval, just as elected officials have been active believers in generating favorable publicity to further their own enterprises (Tedlow, 1979). As a result, efforts to establish and maintain favorable ties with the public have long been a staple of the primary strategies by those in the public arena in terms of business and public service.

As public and private organizations have grown, so, too, have they become more complex. Their "bigness," as Pimlott wrote (1951), has not just been in the form of greater profits or visibility, but also in terms of their publics, including customers, stakeholders, employees, and even competitors. With the emergence of these publics came the need to take steps to ensure little or no gap existed between them and the organization. The result was the hiring of people to provide assistance and guidance to help in this regard. While they may not have been labeled "communicators" in the early years of the American government and well into the 19th century, these bridge builders collectively performed tasks that eventually led to the public relations industry we know today. This evolution, in fact, contributed to the eventual power of the American economy as it solidified an ongoing connection between public and private entities and their publics. It also ensured the importance of the role of communicators in the success of capitalism (Wise, 1980).

Also, rather than being driven by innovative individuals, the role of spokesman gained in prominence more because of an evolving need to create a buffer between the leader and demands on him or her for information, insight, and engagement. While the leader of the organization may want and recognize the need for constant interaction with his or her publics, the reality of his or her responsibilities make it virtually impossible for the leader to personally engage in that interaction as constantly as he or she may want (Hackman & Johnson, 2009). Thus, the time and energy this person does devote to active engagement must be planned and controlled. Coupled with this is the fact that communication, by definition, is dynamic and ever-changing. This speaks to the reality that leaders are being approached by others in ways that did not previously exist or were not as prominent as they once were. This does not even include the responsibilities the chief executive has regarding his or her own job. In the mix of all this is the organizational spokesman. This communicator represents a constant in the swirl in which entity and public both exist and intersect. The spokesman is available and accessible. Such a dynamic is depicted by Barnlund in his transactional model of communication (2008). In this model, the complexity of communication is showcased by recognizing those involved in the communication process as they simultaneously transmit and receive messages. To complicate the dynamic even more, Barnlund notes that when a communication interaction occurs, there are actually six players in the mix: (1) who you think you are, (2) who you think the other person is, (3) who you think the other person thinks you are, (4) who the other person thinks he or she is, (5) who the other person thinks you are, and (6) who the other person thinks you think he or she is.

Imagine the six questions put forth by Barnlund coming together at an intersection, and then imagine being the traffic cop whose job it is to ensure not only that there is not a collision, but that each question is acknowledged and addressed on some level by each of the drivers. This is a daily challenge faced by the organizational spokesman when he or she strives to ensure that the client maintains a healthy relationship with the public every time he or she steps out in front of microphones, cameras, or people with notepads. As a leader within the organization, the spokesman needs to pay as close attention to the messages and information he or she imparts as to the feedback or responses the messages trigger. Furthermore, to help ensure successful exchanges and interactions, the spokesman needs to be vigilant in how he or she behaves, how he or she acts, and how he or she is with others. This is no different than how it is for the leader himself or herself (Hackman & Johnson, 2009). Leadership, whether it comes from the chief executive or the spokesman, is a process whereby an individual influences a group of individuals to achieve a common goal (Northouse, 2007). There is little difference between this definition and the one of public relations put forth recently by the PRSA, which describes it as creating mutually beneficial relationships.

Thus, looking back at the profession of organizational spokesman, there does not exist a string of famous practitioners as one finds in other fields. This is why it is not as easy to trace the evolution of the role of organizational spokesmanship from its beginning days to the present. Rather than using prominent names of the past to trace the trajectory of this communication role, I focus instead on the role itself and the increasing recognition of the need for it. From this perspective, then, the emergence of the organizational spokesman is viewed as an outgrowth of the leadership position itself. Throughout time, the larger or more complex an organization or collection of individuals joined together through shared beliefs or common cause is, the more multifaceted the role of that body's leader is. Whether it has been a large army, tribe, village, community, or business, leaders of any of these entities have found themselves in demanding roles in which they have needed assistants to help carry out their responsibilities and communicate their orders and vision. Of those, the organizational spokesman is among the most important.

Chapter Highlights

- The organizational spokesman is a relatively new phenomenon in communication.
- The organizational spokesman needs to be as familiar with the overall entity as its chief executive is.
- The spokesman can play a key role in helping keep an organization's internal publics unified.
- Amos Kendall is often identified as the first prominent, authorized organizational spokesman in American history.
- The organizational spokesman is a key component in an entity's overall public relations efforts.

Discussion Questions

- How necessary to an organization's overall communication strategies is an organizational spokesman?
- Do you agree with Jerald terHorst's decision to resign as President Ford's press secretary following Ford's decision to pardon Richard Nixon? Why or why not?
- Compare and contrast organizational spokesman and public relations.
- How can and should the organizational spokesman contribute to the entity's public relations efforts?
- Describe the relationship between an organization's top officer and its primary spokesman.

Focus On

Lucy Caldwell, Public Affairs, Fairfax County Police, Fairfax County, Virginia

Lucy Caldwell has more than 20 years of hands-on experience in managing law enforcement and public health incidents. These experiences lend credibility and real-world significance to the numerous media and emergency risk communication sessions she conducts throughout the United States. A recognized expert on developing strategic and tactical communication campaigns, she also helps oversee and implement the social media communication networks for the Fairfax County Police Department in Virginia.

As an active member of the United Prevention Coalition, Caldwell is a leader in helping communities establish dialogues on teen binge drinking. Also, she provides communication training to teens so that they will make a positive difference when they present information about their drug-free lifestyles, whether it is to legislators or to their peers. As part of her work with youth, Caldwell works closely with teens who have been court-ordered to attend mandatory education sessions regarding their drug and/or alcohol violations.

She earned her bachelor's degree at the University of Colorado at Boulder.

Question: How did you get into public relations?

Answer: I studied journalism and communication at the University of Colorado in Boulder. At the time, I was leaning toward some type of work on the environment, perhaps for a publication. I wanted to apply my skills as a writer or some type of communicator. I came back to the Washington, D.C., area and worked for an environmental defense fund as their public relations director. I frequently tell people to follow your heart. Pursue what you are interested in. Life lasts only so long, so you want to devote your time to something that you care about. No matter what you are doing, try to gear your energies to what you are interested in. That first public relations job was not really more than a receptionist's position. It did not pay all that well, either. But if I had not had that title, then I wouldn't have been able to land my first real PR job. It was with the Virginia state police.

This was in the 1980s. It was a grant-funded position, and it gave me an opportunity to try something new. I had not had a lot of experience working in the law enforcement arena. For me, the draw was the people. They were kind, compassionate, and warm. I wanted to be part of that team and help shine a light on them. The state troopers were doing things that were critically important. The officers were involved in some really terrible things, risking their lives in many instances, and were not used to work-ing with an outsider—someone who was not a law officer—like me.

That first job was media oriented. Back then, the media was a lot stronger. There were more reporters, so I had more reporters to deal with. More people were reading newspapers then. And radio stations had more reporters in the field, too. Generally, the media was not as centralized then as it is now. They, of course, still play a very important role when it comes to supplying the public with information and news. I was on call almost 24 hours per day for my nearly 14 years with the state police. I felt [like] part of a family. They knew I supported them. I was there to tell their story. Shine a light on them. Let people know the work the police were doing on behalf of the public.

To me, the most powerful pieces are the ones with the best stories. It's the old saying: "people don't care how much you know until they know how much you care." I wanted to show the public that the police officers cared. The people I worked with then and now (Fairfax County police) are men and women who risk their lives every day. It is a privilege to shine a light on them. I see my work as building relationships. My challenge with the state police—and even now—was to get the troopers to talk to me and include me in what they were doing so [that] I could help tell their stories more effectively. This gave me a chance to be part of something I believed in. I considered it an honor. And I still do. In my current position, one of my strategies is to develop an exchange between law enforcement and the public in a way that portrays the officers as people who work hard at helping others.

There is another key part of my job, too. It involves educating the public. Each year, for example, there are hundreds of new laws passed in Virginia. How can people be held accountable to them unless they know about the laws? As the public information officer, I am in a perfect position to help illustrate the laws—not just for the media but for the general public as well. Different topics. Different audiences. It's an education process. That is how my position has evolved. It is not just about the media but the overall public as well. I see it as a matter of engaging the public. Without that education or informa-tion, people can be confused.

Mainly because of the education element, I see my job as being unusual. I take it as an opportunity to educate or highlight important information for the public and not just promote the police force. Everything I do and attempt to share with the public and media, I first try and address the question of "so what?" How is what I am trying to share important or something they should care about? I take what I do very seriously. So, I have to be accurate. This, of course, is true for everyone in public information, whether or not their job includes serving as a spokesman.

The media is not so much of a presence as it used to be. Still, I view it as being vital to public information work. It is part of our being transparent and open in all that we do. Recently, we organized a program featuring one of our officers who trains young officers who [then] work with impaired drivers. We included reporters in the information aspect of this effort so [that] they could better understand what our officers are working with and need to know.

I try to be a reporter within the agency. Tell the story that goes beyond numbers or statistics. What we say matters to everyone. I try to show [that] officers are not just waiting to put people in jail but are actually trying to help people. Keep them safe. I also try to include our officers in helping plan out our various education programs, too. I try to make what we do seem real and relevant.

At times I use "subject matter experts" to talk with the media rather than doing interviews myself. They are involved in the actual work. Many of these people—the officers—have never done formal interviews with reporters before. If it's appropriate, then I will try and put them out there. Give them positive visibility.

Question: How do you get them to agree to being interviewed by the press? That's not always easy to do.

Answer: First, it begins with building internal relationships. I work at that. With that effort comes trust. And then the officers are more open to working with me and, of course, the media. One of the things I try to do is help the media do their job: tell a good story. This kind of thing helps me feel good. Even more than that, it provides an important service to the public, helps them see [that] the officers are working on their behalf, and helps give the officers some well-deserved recognition.

Question: So, part of your job is not just to work the press, but also to educate the public?

Answer: Absolutely. Recently, we had an inquiry that the use of heroin is on the rise. I had to collect information on this—what I call "data mining." Data mining can be complex, as it involves trying to get the most up-to-date figures or information and then determining how best to present it in a way that is most beneficial to the public. For public relations officers, being thorough and accurate has to come first. Often, in these cases I am able to put the reporter in direct contact with one of our officers. But if that is not possible, then I am in a position to develop talking points and share with the press. I have been given the freedom to do this. When I do put together talking points, I try and work closely with our department's strategic planner so that what I say or what information I share with reporters fits in with that.

Question: Then your responses to the media on any given topic fall under the umbrella of your strategic plan?

Answer: Oh yes. This falls under our effort of being responsive and responsible to the public. That's where helping educate them fits in. What we try to do goes beyond simply enforcing the law. Obviously, as a law enforcement agency, that is a key element. But so are being transparent and being informative. Educating the public is a vital part of our overall strategy. My role is to support that.

Question: Going back to the work you did with the state police, is this where you first started doing work as a spokesman?

Answer: Yes. That began right away. I don't remember at the time thinking all that much about that when I first took the job. Basically, it was explained to me that I would be promoting public safety issues to the public. That included working with the media, providing information to them, and being interviewed by them and quoted. This, of course, was before websites, so we needed the media more to communicate with the public. And then it evolved into my identifying stories and pitching them to the media.

Question: What was being quoted in the paper or being on television like at first?

Answer: I always felt supported by those around me, including my boss. I had the best information I could get, and I always felt confident in what I was sharing.

Question: Are there general guidelines you try to follow when talking with the press?

Answer: There are some mechanical things like eye contact. That's important. Being calm and serious, but human, too. We're not robots. Go beyond a yes or no answer. Explain what you are trying to say. You don't know what the press is going to pick up or highlight, so explain what it is you need to say. There might be something in what you say that makes for a good sound bite. So, be careful with what you say and how you say it, because anything can be used.

Speak in complete sentences. No matter what you are asked, make sure you get your points across. There may be a producer or editor who may be looking at the total piece and draw from something you said, even if it was not in response to a particular question. Reporters, most of them, are good about asking you, "Is there anything else?" This is when you want to drive home your primary points. What is your goal? What do you want them to walk away with? Even if it is an interview you do not want to do. Those can be difficult. But, still, they are important, too. This is why being prepared is so important.

Question: You mentioned earlier the importance of getting your points across. Where do those points come from?

Answer: Before you go into an interview situation, if it is something a subject matter expert can speak to, then you try to bring that person in as quickly as you can. But if it pertains to a more general issue, for example, then you find someone who can give you good feedback on the talking points you put together. In my situation, I come up with the talking points, unless it is specific data. I do not ask my boss what to say. That is my judgment. I let them know what I said and discuss any possible results that may come from it.

The education part of what I do is using the media to talk to the public. Reporters know that. I am always looking for opportunities to do that, even when it involves using an incident as a springboard to inform the public. We need the public, and they need us. The community engagement part of my job has really emerged as a key aspect of what I do. My job as a spokesman is no longer just about the media.

Question: Talk about cultivating the media.
Answer: One strategy I have used is developing a media council that our office meets with on a regular basis. Our conversations were off the record but quite informative for both my office and the press. They pertained to issues the press was covering. Another aspect that has helped in my ties with the press is longevity. You develop a level of trust with certain reporters with whom you have worked for years. And they come to trust you, too. Things are still competitive with the media, so it's a matter of getting to know them and their getting to know me.

I look forward to making my clients—the officers—relevant to the public and to the story that is being covered on any given day. I want the public to know we matter and why, and to know what we are doing as an agency to understand their concerns and then address them. It is rewarding when it all comes together, because you are doing a real service to the public. The key is being consistent and open.

Source: L. Caldwell (personal communication, January, 2012).

Chapter Two

Organizational Role

Communication is all about relationships. It is, in part, about sending or exchanging messages with others. From a broader perspective, it involves a continuous, interactive process of defining and redefining relationships in the context of ever-changing situations (Escudero & Rogers, 2004). Also, any action we take represents a form of communication, even if we are alone when we do it. Words we express and actions we take have impact. In ways that are consequential or small, they make a difference. They change things. A smile, a turn of the head, an innocent greeting, a raised voice, a pronouncement in front of a room of people—all these acts are ones of communication. No matter the intention when we perform them, they affect us and others, sometimes in ways we do not anticipate. This reality is what makes the act of communication so significant and fundamental to our lives. In the case of an organizational spokesman, an act of communication is deliberate and purposeful. While its purpose may range from informing and enlightening to calming and defending, the spokesman's words are set forth much in the way an arrow is by an archer. The words have a target. In addition, they have a purpose. And, finally, they are geared toward a public.

Organizations have a purpose, too. Some strive to make money. Some seek to provide a service to the public without regard for profit. In each case, they employ workers and attempt to interact with various publics. These interactions carry with them the purpose of sustained connection. For-profit organizations want customers, while nonprofit entities work toward expanding the number of clients that benefit from their service. Despite these differences, they, too, are in the relationship business. They desire visibility, a positive reputation, and respectability. Each shares a need for those who can help them achieve and maintain these qualities. Professional communicators can do this. They can play a key role in the organization's survival and possible growth by helping devise strategies to establish ties with various publics and then maintain them. In the case of the spokesman, it is a matter of where and how best this professional fits in. How much of a role does he or she play in helping these two kinds of organizations achieve their overriding objectives?

In the context of this dynamic, at times members of an organization do not always see how they are perceived by those external to their entity. As the organization's "face" or "voice," the spokesman is regularly in the position of interacting with external publics. As a result, he or she can serve as a two-way mirror that helps generate important awareness for his or her fellow internal members. This link helps ensure a level of openness that, in turn, generates transparency on behalf of the organization and greater teamwork among its members (Krone, 2005). By playing such a role, the spokesman helps set in motion a public relations style geared toward encouraging a two-way flow of communication (Grunig, 1989). This current state is relatively new in the evolution of communication as a recognized social science. Generally, the value of public relations to an organization's sustained success, in times of normality and crisis, has grown, particularly as a result of technological advances that have helped make reaching out to others easier and less costly (Newsom, Turk, & Kruckeberg, 2013). As a rule, the public relations function exists for the sole purpose of supporting the overall mission of the organization.

In many ways, such a reality also applies to an organization's leader. How well the leader communicates helps determine his or her effectiveness and, in many ways defines his or her style of leadership. For instance, an early study by Lewin, Lippitt, and White (1939) examined a range of leaders and concluded that there are three primary types of leaders: authoritarian, democratic, and laissez-faire. In terms of how leaders communicate, the researchers found that the authoritarian leader tends to engage in one-way, downward communication in which he or she controls discussions with subordinates. A democratic leader is found to involve his or her followers in two-way, open communication. This person's focus is more on equal interaction. A third type of leader—laissez-faire—tends to avoid interaction with staff. The publics on the radar screen of the leaders are the same as those in the sights of the spokesman. However, the spokesman's style of interacting with staff throughout the organization does not necessarily mirror that of the leader. From a practical perspective, the spokesman lacks the organizational authority to present himself or herself as having power over others. From a professional standpoint, as the spokesman needs to establish and maintain positive ties with colleagues, his or her interactions need to be approached more as a collaboration of equals.

Regardless of the size or exact setting of an organization, the bottom-line responsibility of the chief executive officer within an organization is to make the entity as effective as possible. As dissected by J. Grunig, L. Grunig, and Dozier (2002), what makes an organization effective is its ability to attain goals, the level of interdependence among its members, the degree to which its various constituencies are used strategically, and the strength of the connection between those constituencies and the organization's values.

As part of this, another important challenge the leaders of an entity have is what to do with their communicators. How best can the organization's communication arm be utilized to help the entity achieve its highest level of effectiveness? This decision, however, goes beyond simply determining where the director of public relations, for example, belongs on the organizational chart. The real determining factor made by those leaders sensitive to the importance of communicator is how best can those professionals be utilized to enhance the organizations various relationships in a way that feeds into meeting its goals? Leaders want their employees to work in harmony, be productive, and feel good about what they do and where they work. They also want external publics to think positive thoughts about them. And they are in the business of persuasion and influencing others (Hersey, 1984). In order for the overriding goals to be achieved, leaders realize that it takes more than their ability make pronouncements, bark out orders, or set policy. The leaders need support in this regard. Communicators can and should be part of this mix. In fact, they are in a unique position here because their primary purpose is to influence others as well (Seitel, 1984). If leadership is viewed as partnership with followers (Block, 1993), communication is also an act assessed by the followers it, too, generates. More to the point, because communication is an evolving system, who best to be directly involved with helping prepare and facilitate the messaging this entails than the communication professional (Rogers, 1972)?

Historically, communication, no matter the targeted public, is grounded in relationships and relational activity (Kennan & Hazelton, 2006). Given that, it is imperative that an organization's external and internal outreach efforts be in sync. We all know the cliché about the right hand not knowing what the left hand is doing. Taken literally, this suggests that the two hands are not working in harmony but, instead, are going about their own business, with little to no regard for what the other is doing. In such a scenario, it would not take long for the two to end up competing with each other or giving the owner of the two hands a giant headache—or both. Whatever the result, the ultimate outcome is a person who is neither productive nor happy. Applying such a state to an organization, one would see a struggling entity that is operating with little strategic sense and certainly with little chance of obtaining anything close to sustained success.

This, then, speaks to how important it is for organizations to have a strong public relations function. But it is only strong when it operates in total compliance with the organization's overall vision or mission. These visions represent how organizations wish to be seen, and professional communicators are hired to ensure this happens. In their research, J. Grunig, L. Grunig, and Dozier (2002) found that for the public office to be truly good if not excellent, it must possess these elements: (a) be headed by a manager who conceptualizes and directs the public relations programs, (b) be staffed by professionals who have the knowledge needed to be managers, and (c) provide all staff members with equal opportunity to occupy the managerial position. Thus, to be as good as it can be, the public relations office needs to be staffed with the best possible people, with each having the ability and opportunity to assume a director-level position. These professionals, in the context of an organization and its relationships, must strive to control mutuality, or the degree to which parties connect, establish, and maintain trust, achieve mutual satisfaction, maintain mutual commitment to their relationship, and keep their exchanges active and timely (Hon & Grunig, 1999).

As a professional communicator, the organizational spokesman has a definitive role to play here, no matter whether he or she is in charge of the communication operation or simply a member of its team. For the spokesman to be removed or separated from the organization's total public relations efforts would be a detriment to the spokesman position as well as to the communication team. On the one hand, being separate from the communication office or unit would tend to keep the spokesman in the dark or in a position of ignorance on various issues that he or she might be called on to discuss in public forums. Thus, being separate from an organization's communication unit could potentially compromise the effectiveness of the spokesman. On the other hand, such a separation could also potentially compromise the effectiveness of the communication unit if it is unaware of what information the spokesman is passing along to the media and members of the outside public. Image building for any organization is challenge enough without the members of the entity's communication professionals carrying out their duties separately or with a minimal degree of coordination (D'Alessandro, 1991).

In terms of an organization's inner workings, what is it that the organizational spokesman does to help the entity achieve its primary goals? Where and how does this professional fit in when it comes to connecting with the entity's higher-ranking officers, as well as with its mid- and lower-level employees? In essence, other than giving interviews or talking with the media, what does the organizational spokesman do when he or she is not speaking on behalf of the client or company? Is the spokesman an island who works independently from others, or someone who works closely with their internal colleagues and the external public as a matter of day-to-day routine? The purpose of this chapter is to explore these questions from both a routine perspective as well as during times of crisis or disruption.

Generally, the spokesman's place within the organization is twofold: external and internal. Even though the spokesman may be perceived as being one-dimensional in the sense that he or she contends only with publics external to the organization, the reality of the position is different. The spokesman's feet, in short, are placed in both camps. For the spokesman to be effective at his or her primary function, he or she must have a thorough understanding and awareness of the inner workings of that which they represent to the outside public. This means that the spokesman's ties to and depth of knowledge of the organization's component parts must be strong. There are few things that do more harm to a spokesman's reputation or to the organization's image than someone who speaks to a public from a position of ignorance. Such a scenario places the spokesman's reputation as a credible representative in jeopardy. To delve into this matter in greater depth, a detailed examination of the spokesman's internal and external ties and role is in order.

Internal Relations

In this discussion of the spokesman's role within the organization, it is important to distinguish between the general role of communication as a function and the role of the spokesman as a specific staff member. Obviously, any comparison produces a great deal of overlap. That, I might note, is a good thing, as is acknowledges the overlapping challenges that come with addressing both internal and external publics. But a comparison also highlights the fact that the spokesman, at best, performs only a portion of the communication function. After all, organizations possess a number of communication needs, which range from producing promotional material to striving to pitch stories to the media to even overseeing internal communiqués. Given that, it is not my intent here to place too much emphasis on the overall communication function, but rather to zero in on what the spokesman does or does not do. At the risk of making this any more complicated than it needs to be, it should be said that the exact duties or responsibilities of the spokesman are often determined by the organization's size and the vision of the chief executive. Another factor making it difficult to generalize too much here—but still worth noting—is how the chief executive perceives both communication as a function and spokesmanship as a specific role. In running or overseeing their organizations, executives have the challenge of determining how best to do this and the role communication plays in their efforts. This entails melding communication strategies with cognitive control processes (Jordan, 1993). Thus, important variables are present that help determine the organization's overall communication effort and strategies.

An analysis of the spokesman's internal relations touches on three parts: where the position belongs, the position's role, and the position's day-to-day interactions or relationship with others. While these points overlap, dissecting each separately helps provide a more complete portrait of the role of the organizational spokesman position itself. It is also worth noting that the spokesman's internal interactions are geared to complement his or her external efforts. To start, one common thread that runs through each rests on the extent to which the executive determines the spokesman should be involved in internal communication. Misplacing the entity's most visible communicator could compromise the in-house flow of interaction and information sharing. Incorrect judgment on the executive's part could, in fact, do harm to communication focus and process (Cappella, 1983). After all, the chief officer wants effective internal communication but primarily wants to support the organization's ability to achieve maximum profit and meet other goals. This includes creating an environment that brings out the best in each worker (Snyder, 1987) as well as one that fosters trust and consistent collaboration (Edmondson, 2006). Furthermore, establishing a framework for leadership communication in which the structure's communication team, including the spokesman, helps foster the entity's values and mission among its employees and members helps create a more tight-knit internal dynamic (Huber & Boyle, 2005).

Positioning the Spokesman

Any time we acquire a nice piece of furniture or artwork, the challenge of where to put it immediately comes to the forefront. The solution to this question is twofold: what makes the most sense to the overall room or structure as well as what best showcases the item itself. In many ways, it is no different with the role of organizational spokesman. The result is seeking answers to a string of fundamental questions: Where does the official spokesman fit within the organization? To whom should this person report? To what office or department should this person belong? Or should they not be part of any specific office at all and, instead, be a lone wolf who is kind of a like a freelance employee, whose only ties to others are situational in nature rather than part of a day-to-day, predetermined structure? In dealing with these questions, it is important to remember that at a minimum the spokesman is part of the organization's communication arm. Obviously, it is a key part.

Thus, for any organization to succeed, one of the needed ingredients is to have a communication element producing communiqués that are timely, informative, accurate, and pertinent to their designated audiences. The purpose of this aspect of the organization is twofold: to properly facilitate communicate efforts in a well-coordinated manner compatible with the organization's internal structure, and to represent the organization in a manner that supports and educates others about its values, policies, initiatives, programs, and successes. Ultimately, an organization's communication arm should support what Taylor (1911) viewed as the entity's trinity of needed characteristics: efficiency of operation, monetary success, and control of actions. The spokesman needs to be actively involved in this effort, particularly as it applies to the organization's internal dynamic. The reason for this speaks directly to the spokesman's primary responsibility of representing his or her organization before the public. The spokesman needs to be well versed in the organization's various communication overtures—internal and external. This is made all the easier if the spokesman is actually involved in the devising and/or planning of initiatives designed to enhance these initiatives.

Role of the Spokesman

One of the fundamental traits of a professional communicator is that he or she operates with the public in mind. Of course, this person must never lose sight of the client, either. As communication is an act of impacting and/or connecting with others, the person with this responsibility does not have the luxury of operating with only one public or the other in mind. That comes with being in the relationship business. This, then, is why the organization's communication arm should be regularly and visibly involved with as many aspects of the entity as possible. Even more plainly, the spokesman needs to help remind the internal and external publics that each exists and is taking an active interest in the other (Deatherage & Hazelton,1998). More to the point, as the nature of the spokesman's role is that he or she be a key link between the organization and its outside publics, this particular communicator needs to be an active internal player as a way of reminding workers that their work impacts others. The spokesman should also possess the ability to balance the discussions and decisions made internally by the entity's leaders with the challenge of presenting them to the external public in a manner that does not violate internal confidences or compromise vital strategies (Trist, 1981). If organizations are, in fact, organic wholes that interact dynamically with their various environments (Morgan, 1998), the spokesman can and should be a key player in helping maintain a viable linkage between each. This is particularly important when one recognizes the reality that change is constantly being thrust on organizations by an array of variables ranging from competitors and evolving technology to economic challenges and personnel demands. This, in essence, is part of a management complexity theory that sees change as being as constant of a companion of organization as it is to individuals (McMaster, 1996).

Specifically, the spokesman should be the ever-present "fly on the wall" at meetings deemed important by the leaders. The content of these meetings can range from gatherings where policies are set, organizational goals are debated and established, or solutions to events affecting the overall entity are sought. This communicator needs to hear the debate and be witness to how leaders reach various decisions. Why this is important is because such deliberations may ultimately end up being of interest to the external public. As in all likelihood it will be the spokesman's job to explain and respond to questions about those kind of decisions, the more background and understanding he or she has about them, the better this person will be able to address them to properly represent the organization. At such meetings, it is also appropriate for the spokesman to be part of the conversation, particularly if he or she is recognized as a vital part of the organization's dominant group of deciders. Ideally, this would be the case. If not, someone with an expertise in communication should be involved. To the external public and even to the organization's workforce, the spokesman can serve as a stabilizing presence who represents a continuity on the entity's part to maintain its commitment to the many who rely on it.

An example of this is found in 2000, when two health systems—Holy Cross Health System and Mercy Health Services—announced their intention to consolidate. Initially, members of both systems were not favorable or comfortable with what they viewed as a disruption and possible threat to coverage they were receiving. A joint public relations team was created and immediately organized a number of focus groups to address concerns and share information on the benefits of this move. In addition, in working with their members and stakeholders, the two systems spoke with one voice in the form of key spokesmen who were given the tools and resources needed to properly explain the merger. The result was that what began as a high level of skepticism on the part of those affected was turned into an even higher level of support.

One reality of any role a professional plays within his or her organization pertains to the power he or she has within that entity. How well or easily can or should the spokesman be able to make others do what he or she wants (Weber, 1946)? What is the spokesman's level of authority over others? How much direct influence does he or she possess over others? Generally, it is common for many to judge the importance of themselves and others based on how much direct control they have over others. In the case of the spokesman, such a characteristic is not all that necessary. The spokesman's internal role is more subtle. It rests far more on the ability to connect with others, gain their confidence, and collaborate, rather than simply how many people the spokesman can and does boss around. In a broad sense, then, the internal role of the spokesman is one of empowerment, a multidimensional social process that helps people gain control over their own lives (Page & Czuba, 1999). Specifically, the so-called power a spokesman has within the organization is more fluid, as it speaks to his or her interactions with others versus his or her direct authority and ability to foster change, particularly as it might apply to specific situations.

Day-to-Day Interactions

For any organization to remain viable, its internal "home" must be sound. Specifically, the foundation of the dynamic between management and the subordinates needs to be one that is positive. Though he was not talking about internal relations within public and private organizations, Abraham Lincoln stated it best in his famous 1858 "house divided" speech. "A house divided against itself cannot stand," he said (Fehrenbacher, 1960). To survive and be successful, an entity must maintain a certain level of coordination and collegiality. Of course, such a relationship, even in organizations that enjoy a high level of morale, is never easy (Kennan & Hazelton, 2006). Internal public relations in the form of newsletters, town hall meetings, broad emails, annual reports, and other traditional forms of communiqués, is generally acknowledged as being a contributing factor to creating a "house" without significant division (Kennan & Hazelton, 2006). By making a point of connecting with others at all levels of the organization, the spokesman can help serve as both a representative of management and an advocate of the workforce. This helps support the focus of message exchange, which is the essence of organizational communication (Buzzawell & Stohl, 1999). In addition, the spokesman can be a vessel or channel of information flow between the two levels. Doing so helps keep the organization and its members locked into a process through which they act together and create, sustain, and manage meanings through a range of verbal and nonverbal signs within a particular context (Conrad, 1993).

As we have already touched on, how one leads often contributes to how he or she communicates with those who report to him or her. Past research studies have found that those in management tend to view their workers as approaching their jobs with two distinct styles: as not wanting to work and therefore needing to be led with little regard for individual needs, and as seeking work as the way to achieve greater fulfillment (McGregor, 1960). Brought out in McGregor's Theory X management and Theory Y management study, these perspectives also point to differences in leadership styles, which, in turn, suggest variances in how internal communication is carried out. No matter the style, however, leaders seek to exercise a certain level of control over their subordinates (Ellis, 1979). The result is that subordinates tend to demonstrate some level of compliance with their leaders as they carry out their duties (Watson, 1982). While such a dynamic may help define the interaction between the leader and subordinate, it does not lessen the important role the communicator can play in helping that relationship be one that is both positive and productive.

As a viable member of the organization's team, the spokesman is an active participant in the interactions and collaborations between workers that occur on a daily basis. It goes without saying that this interaction is critical to the organization's ultimate success. Such a dynamic speaks to the social capital within the organization and just how much of an asset each worker, regardless of station or position, is (Leanna & Van Buren, 1999). This social capital refers to the organization's ability to create, maintain, and ultimately make use of internal relationships to achieve its goals (Portes, 1998). As an active and very visible member of the organization, the spokesman can use his or her prominence by working with managers and other leaders to encourage and help foster greater comradery among the workers, even as it occurs in the context of constant change (Fairhurst & Putnam, 1998).

One other point regarding internal relations in terms of how it is carried out in a crisis situation: we will cover this later in the text, but it should be noted that the spokesman should never forget the importance of those men and women who comprise the organization (Argenti, 2002). Yes, the media needs to be dealt with, and so, too, does the general public. But those who are on the payroll or do volunteer work on behalf of the organization should never, ever be overlooked. Their need to know runs second to no other group. Employees need to be kept abreast of what has happened or is happening and how the circumstances affect them. Keeping these people well informed shows respect and regard and helps ensure their loyalty in good and rocky times. Furthermore, the spokesman should help ensure that the organization is sensitive to its employees by providing counseling and access to medical authorities should they be needed in times of crisis (Coombs, 2007b). This kind of communication helps provide employees and members with a stronger sense of organizational identity that adds much to internal morale (Krone & Morgan, 2000).

External Relations

In 2003, the City of San Jose San Jose Public Library, San Jose State University and San Jose State University Library (keep as it) introduced the new Dr. Martin Luther King, Jr. Library, the first joint library in the United States between a major university and large city (Hendrix & Hayes, 2007). As exciting as this venture was, it also generated a good deal of skepticism about how it would work. As a result of a strong public relations effort under the umbrella of specific talking points, nearly 30 targeted audiences were identified and communicated with, and messages were sent out to members of the general public in which the benefits of this initiative were emphasized. Media coverage proved to be quite positive and public acceptance was universal. In addition, nearly $0.5 million was raised among sponsors and active donors.

The key to the King library event and any successful public relations effort is seen in how well the communication team is able to bring together the needs of the public with those of the organization (Ledingham, 2000). In this regard, *public relations* is defined as a management function that establishes and maintains mutually beneficial relationships between an organization and the public on whom its success or failure depends (Cutlip, Center & Broom, 1994). As was and is the case regarding the organization's internal relations, the spokesman is a key element as what he or she does pertains to external relations. In fact, with the possible exception of the chief executive officer, the spokesman is the one person who can help assure the public that its needs are very much a priority of the organization. Failing to do so in all likelihood will contribute to a loss of confidence in the organization on the part of the public and a likely shift in their desire to utilize the services or products of that entity.

Public relations, as we have mentioned, revolves around the establishment and maintenance of relationships. Relationship management, as this is otherwise known, speaks to the essence of communication and to the work of those who dwell in it, including spokesmen (Ledingham & Bruning, 2000a). Thus, in the realm of external relations, it is the dual challenge of the spokesman to not just articulate information or a particular message but to do so in a way that enhances the organization's ties with its public. This includes distinctive publics as well. Examples of these groups would be retired people, single parents, or those belonging to a specific political party. Serving as a main conduit for successful ties with the external public places the spokesman in the unique position of being their organization's ears and eyes. The spokesman is the constant front man or woman. As a result, the spokesman is the basket into which the questions, concerns, musings, and so forth of the public, including the media, are tossed. As best the spokesman can, he or she responds to or answers all that is directed toward him or her. The discerning public takes their cues from the verbal and nonverbal signals the spokesman transmits. Is this always fair? Probably not. Does this make the job of spokesman all the more complex? Without question. Together, this reality makes the job of spokesman the most unique among his or her fellow communication professionals. The spokesman, via his or her public pronouncements, can actually influence an organization's positions or directions on an issue, whereas a traditional media relations director does not. This type of professional communicator tends to work in the background or behind those whose position requires they be more out front. Examples of these kind of organizational members can range from the chief executive officer to those being highlighted for their achievement or expertise.

As part of that, here is a not-so-hypothetical question for the reader: Suppose a question is asked of the spokesman that he or she does not know the answer to? What should the spokesman do? How should he or she respond? Should he or she give an educated guess? Is it advisable to say, "No comment"? The answer to these questions is no. The spokesman should never try to guess at a response or answer. When that is attempted, the result usually is not good. Either the person ends up giving out incorrect, misleading, or incomplete information, thus creating confusion, or ends up doing harm to his or her own credibility and, ultimately, poorly representing the organization. If one does not know the answer to an inquiry, he or she is encouraged and urged to admit it. Do not make something up or take an educated guess. While it is OK to not know the answer to everything that might be asked, it is not OK to pretend you do. Granted, standing in front of a room full of reporters creates a certain element of pressure that makes one feel that he or she needs to come up with some kind of answer. Do not fall into that trap. Not only is it all right to say you do not know the answer to something; it is acceptable and smart. "I don't know, but I'll see what I can find out and get back to you" is the perfect response when something like this happens. Generally, the public is fair and does not expect spokesmen to know literally everything that is asked of them. But what they do expect—and rightfully so—is honesty. While no one wants to be viewed as not knowing all the facts about something, this far outweighs being known as someone who does not speak truth. Credibility, once lost, is nearly impossible to recapture.

So much of the spokesman's role revolves around projecting and safeguarding a positive image of the organization rather than what one views as being the more traditional duty of attempting to generate greater publicity for that which a person represents. As much as is possible, it is actually to the organization's advantage to keep these responsibilities separate. In building a communication team, the organization should have a spokesman work separately from the media or public relations worker. While it is true that the effort of both speaks largely to external relations, in specific terms the spokesman seeks to bolster and enhance the entity's image and reputation to the press and general public, while the public relations worker is largely managing press relations, pitching stories, and devising ways to bolster the entity's visibility and public profile. Thus, from a general perspective, the responsibility of helping maintain the organization's positive external relations is a worthy challenge for any professional. The challenge is amplified when viewed in the context of media relations and crisis communication. Our next step is to examine these two vital areas more closely but first with a key point. Both the spokesman and the media relations professional function under the organization's overriding strategies, but with a significant difference. The spokesman tends to represent the organization's policy-level decisions that represent its grand strategy (Botan, 2006). The media relations director is more tied to campaign-level efforts that support the grand strategy.

Media Relations

Make no mistake: the organizational spokesman and members of the press have a special relationship. It is different from the relationship between the press and more traditional public relations officers or publicists. As much as is realistically possible, the spokesman needs to project an image of being removed from the fray of pitching stories to the media. This is largely unlike the public relations director, for instance, who devotes the bulk of his or her energies toward finding and/or shaping stories to bring to the attention of the press so that reporters and editors will find them interesting and compelling. In more blunt terms, this person's role is more of an overt salesperson or pitchman. His or her tasks include writing press releases and e-mail pitches and assisting with press conferences at which the spokesman is the featured speaker or, at least, is among the featured speakers (Guth & Marsh, 2012). On the other hand, the spokesman seeks to project more of a persona in which he or she is viewed as being removed from the day-to-day efforts of seeking publicity. This is important, as it puts this professional, much like the chief executive officer, in a position of being viewed as one who is more objective and even credible in his or her comments and analysis of the organization and its overall efforts. (Obviously, it is understood the chief executive officer and the spokesman are doing all they can to promote their organization—much like the public relations director. The primary difference here is one of perception. The public relations director is more blatant is his or her promotional efforts.) Whether it is the spokesman or public relations agent, both interact with a media that is far different than it used to be. This new media, as labeled by Wilkinson, Grant, and Fisher (2013) have the ability now to tell stories in a manner that enhances straight reporting of facts or information. Parallel to this, largely due to current technological realities, today's audiences have more sources of news and information, audience participation in the news is greater, and news itself is reported much more quickly (Stovall, 2012).

Thus, the spokesman is similar to the editor of the local newspaper or television station who is involved in day-to-day news but also tries to view things from a broader, big-picture perspective. The role of the two—spokesman and editor—is to look for trends and turns in the road that their publics are taking in regard to the organization. They are kindred spirits perched in high chairs. When the spokesman and editor connect, their conversation often revolves around projections, analysis, and broad perspectives. They also discuss specific events or singular stories, but this is generally a topic more likely suited to publicists and reporters. Yes, they are interested in those things, too, but, generally, each wants to assess the place of those stories within a more grand vision. Being able to do so enables them to better speak to or report individual stories.

The editor interacts with public relations agents who seek greater visibility for their clients much as the spokesman interacts with individual reporters in search of quotable comments and reliable information. This is a large part of their day-to-day jobs and are aspects that help define their level of competence and effectiveness. The two are fellow agenda shapers in the context of carrying out their responsibilities from different camps. This is an intriguing dynamic in the world of spokesmanship. While the spokesman may not have quite the direct influence an editor has in determining what stories to cover, feature, and bring before the public, the spokesman is part of that mix from a perch that is not like any other in the profession of communications or public relations.

The two communicators are also currently operating in a world—in terms of their profession—that is different than it used to be. With the advent of social media, the reach of both public relations professionals and journalists is far more diverse than it ever was. Plus, the public itself is more actively involved in the spreading of information—again, thanks to social media. News is reported and distributed at a much faster and more immediate clip, and interaction with the public is greater. These trends have led researchers to label our current era as convergent journalism (Wilkinson, Grant, & Fisher, 2013). While this dynamic certainly applies to journalism, it also applies to public relations. Professionals from both camps have multiple distribution channels or avenues at their disposal, including print, broadcast, message boards, and digital signage. Collectively, they enable the journalists and public relations practitioners to more easily and directly interact with various publics. This new reality has had a significant impact on the relationship between the two types of communicators. Social media has presented public relations practitioners with more ways to communicate directly with targeted publics, thus making them not as dependent on the media for publicity or greater visibility as they once were.

Nevertheless, spokesmen must tread lightly when it comes to their interactions with the press. This is largely because of the inevitable tension between public relations and the press and the role both play in communication outreach. The spokesman's role is largely one of reaction. It is the publicist who is far more proactive in reaching out to the media. The key to the spokesman's success lies in the preparation (Wilcox & Reber, 2013). As the voice and/or face of an organization, it is essential that this person do all he or she can to avoid or minimize missteps when it comes to making comments to the press. As we have suggested, making false or inaccurate comments can do harm to the organization's overall image and perceived viability. One way to do this, particularly when one is approached by reporters for comments on a particular issue, is to try to get a sense of what ʾspecifically the reporters wish to know and ask about. The spokesman should do this before agreeing to a formal, on-the-record interview. The more a reporter's motive and goals are known, the better able the spokesman will be able to couch or frame his or her comments in response to questions asked of them.

Much of the time reporters and editors now spend their time processing information rather than gathering it (Wilcox & Reber, 2013). Much of this information comes from public relations officers, including spokesmen. By the same token, as the public relations types strive to promote, persuade, and serve as advocates for clients, they then rely on journalists to give their messages and efforts greater credibility and more visibility. Thus, even with the exciting technology of today, the two continue to depend on each other. They have, in essence, evolved into uneasy and reluctant partners.

This leads to a word about on-the-record and off-the-record interactions with the media. There are different schools of thought on this among spokesman and communication professionals. Some feel that it is all right to go off the record with reporters when matters of sensitivity are being discussed or background information is being shared. When spokesmen make this request or state that they will discuss something only off the record, they are, in essence, drawing a line in the sand, which says that anything stated after that point by them is not for publication, attribution, or reporting. The great majority of reporters who agree to such a request honor it. (Sometimes a reporter does not agree to this request. When this happens, the spokesman needs to adjust his or her comments accordingly.) But, assuming the reporter agrees to the spokesman's request, if the spokesman then proceeds to reveal something that, in the judgment of the reporter, is newsworthy, the reporter will inevitably find a way to attain a public disclosure of that information. Rarely do such off-the-record comments remain secret for long (McIntyre, 2009).

In my years as a spokesman, I rarely attempted to go off the record with any reporters. I always found it easier to treat every conversation or interaction as if it were a matter of public conception. In other words, I was always "on." My thinking was, why put either myself or the reporter in the potential position of having to later tiptoe around sensitive topics or contend with direct on-the-record questions that reporters would invariably ask based on what I had privately disclosed earlier? Also, I continue to believe always being on the record adds to the credibility of what comments I do make. Plus, it does not tempt reporters to violate an off-the-record agreement should newsworthy information be disclosed.

Finally, in the spokesman's dance with reporters, a summary of helpful tips to keep in mind as articulated by blogger Phillips (2011) has been put forth. They range from deciding on two or three important points of information to emphasize, answering questions directly, and not hesitating to repeat the message to maintaining an open tone that is not defensive, being engaging and not robotic, and avoiding jargon-filled language. The objective of the spokesman when talking with a reporter is to be understood, not to make a friend. This is not to say that one cannot enjoy his or her connection with reporters and fall into friendly and fun banter with them. (To paraphrase the old punch line: "some of my best friends are reporters.") But no matter how well a spokesman gets on with reporters, even to the point of becoming personal friends, the spokesman should never take off his or her "business hat" when talking about business or work-related matters. The bottom line in this type of scenario is that spokesmen have a job to do and so, too, do reporters.

There is also a second vital "bottom line" when it comes to spokesman-press relations. The spokesman, at best, has only a modicum or moderate level of control over the end result of the message he or she wishes to communicate to the public (Zoch & Molleda, 2006). Yes, the spokesman controls the message he or she is speaking or transmitting, but what the spokesman does not control is how reporters will use it, how they will interpret it, or even whether they will ignore it. The reporter and his or her editor ultimately decide the exact wording, context, and public release time and day of information passed onto them by a spokesman. It is not always immediate, nor is it always in the context in which the spokesman initially intends. If one believes in a free press, as I do, this is how it should be. However, what should be does not necessarily make the spokesman's job any easier. In one regard, this reality pictures the role and life of a spokesman as one of opposite dynamics. On the one hand, the well-prepared spokesman is in control of his or her output. The spokesman has a sense of what is going to be asked of him or her and, just as important, he or she knows what he or she is going to say to those inquiries. The result is a sense of assurance and even confidence. On the other hand, the spokesman does not and cannot dictate or determine what will happen to his or her words or statements. The results here are feelings of anxiety and insecurity. At least from a professional standpoint, the spokesman certainly dwells in a schizophrenic world (Hayes, Hendrix, & Jumar, 2013). This world, it should be noted, is one in which communication is ongoing and comes from reality rather than simply reflects reality (Deetz, 1982).

Such a setting for this kind of uncertainty on the spokesperson's part is the press or news conference. Generally, as a communication tool, press conferences should be used sparingly and only for the biggest or most significant of occasions. When an organization schedules a press conference, it is signaling to the media that it has a big and newsworthy announcement to make. Even though the spokesperson knows what he or she is going to say going into the press conference, he or she has little idea how what he or she says will be reported. Such is the nature of press interaction. The media attention the spokesman will be receiving from this kind of event is uncontrolled (Moore & Warren, 1992).

Given that the spokesman cannot control how his or her messages and statements will be interpreted in written or spoken form, what steps can the spokesman take to maintain at least some level of control when it comes to communicating messages to the public via the media? A solution is found in the three legs of what Zoch-Molleda (2006) depicts as a model of media relations. The three parts are framing, information subsidies, and agenda building. Collectively, they provide spokesmen with a road map toward coming at least close to controlling how their messages are communicated to the public.

Framing

One important first step toward this end is found in the word *framing*. Goffman (1974) defines it as a schemata of interpretation through which individuals organize and make sense of information or an occurrence. Perhaps in their best form, framed messages call attention to certain aspects of a reality. As the same time, a particular frame also draws attention away from other aspects of reality (Entman, 1993). One example of this might be the political spokesman who stresses that his client voted for a strong defense budget but against proposed allocations for a cleaner environment. This spokesman wants only certain information to be reported. It, of course, is always interesting to watch those moments when spokesman and reporters "battle" over which aspect should or will be the focus of attention. One might find it similar to watching a mongoose go head-to-head with a cobra. While the mongoose usually wins, whether it is the spokesman or reporter in that role varies.

Framing is an integral occurrence within all communication outreach. In essence, it represents the establishment of common frames of reference about topics or issues of interest to specific people or the general public (Hallahan, 1999). The spokesman is the organization's most visible if not key framer of messages. From his or her perspective, the purposes of this to define problems, identify causes, make judgments about a situation that is causing a challenge or problem, or suggest remedies or treatments for the problem (Entman, 1993).

Information Subsidies

Information subsidies, the second leg of the stool, speak to the prepackaged information spokesmen use to help communicate or distribute their messages. The essential purpose of these packets is to increase the odds of the information prepared by them being con-sumed and/or utilized by the media and general public (Gandy, 1982). If this happens, the spokesman or media representative has successfully increased the odds that what reporters draw from in the writing and/or broadcasting of their stories is what has been handed to them by the organization's voice/face.

A common term for these subsidies is *press kit*. As public relations as evolved, so, too, has the press kit. In many ways it is as commonplace at a public or media event as the spokesman himself or herself. Often press kits are prepared for notable events (Wilcox & Reber, 2013). They are designed to provide reporters with assistance in their coverage of an event. In addition, they make available background information on the sponsor of the event. On all counts, the press kit represents the attempt by public relations professionals, including the spokesman, to control the information from which reporters will be drawing to do their stories. Specifically, press kits can and do include such items as a press release on the event; brief biographies of the participants; pertinent photos; a fact sheet on the product, organization, and event; and a relevant brochure or two. In my years at George Mason University, press kits have been a regular part of the outreach arsenal. At the institution's annual commencement ceremony, for example, the press kit includes a detailed press release on the event, copies of the speeches being given by the commencement and student speakers, quality photos of the two as well as ones of people being individually honored, fact sheets on the graduating class and the university, and a brochure outlining highlights of the institution's academic year. Nowadays, public relations practitioners are producing digital press kits for the same purpose. In either case, these information subsidies comple-ment statements on the event at hand by the designated spokesman.

With the exchange between spokesman and press comes several questions: How effective are these information subsidies? How well do they work? How much do they actually assist the spokesman in what he or she is trying to do? Are they of help to the press? From a practitioner's standpoint, I can report that they can and do serve as helpful tools that complement the spoken words of the spokesman. In terms of research on this topic, scholars have found that information subsidies do enhance the news value of the efforts of both the spokesman and media relations practitioner (Zoch & Molleda, 2006). Interestingly, this is despite the fact that many reporters and editors generally recognize prepackage communiqués to the press as being self-serving and in need of rewriting (Martin & Singletary, 1981).

Agenda Building

This concept was introduced by McCombs and Shaw (1972) in an attempt to explain the news media's impact on public opinion information (Zoch & Molleda, 2006). Their initial findings in the introduction of this process revolved around politics. Depending on the media's emphasis on various campaign issues, the judgment of voters as to what they viewed as being important and timely was affected, McCombs and Shaw said. However, on a more broad scale, the implication was that the media helped shape public opinion on matters beyond the realm of politics. This was the premise of the hypodermic needle model of communication first articulated back in the 1930s. Also known as the magic bullet theory of mass communication, it spoke to the media's direct influence over public interest and public actions (Berger, 1995).

This theory of mass communication was followed by what was called the two-step flow theory. In this theory, the heavy role of the media in influencing the public agenda continued to be acknowledged (Katz, 1955). The difference from the previous theory was the role of public opinion leaders as an added source of influence over the public. These theories, though not mentioned much in today's communication world, still cast a giant shadow when it comes to explaining what motivates public opinion and/or actions. Without question, the fingerprints of the media continue to be seen in all that the public thinks and does. To add to this, Lang and Lang (1981) suggest that the agenda-building process driven by the media is a continuous one involving a number of feedback loops as perpetuated by both the press and professional communicators. These so-called professional communicators include spokespeople who articulate demands and positions and either demand or strive for media attention.

One logical conclusion here is that within many organizations the spokesman, on behalf of his or her client, has evolved into becoming a key player in helping shape the public agenda. The spokesman's level of influence is determined in large measure by his or her success in working with the media, level of professional credibility, and ability to generate media interest when making public pronouncements of some sort. There is also the matter of accessibility. One of the qualities reporters like most about their sources is that they have a high level of accessibility. Are their sources a simple phone call or e-mail away? Do they returns calls in a timely manner and then respect whatever deadlines under which the reporter might be working? Spokesman who are able to do this get high marks on any reporter's likeability chart. For the spokesman, of course, this often means placing the reporter's needs and responsibilities over his or her own. It means, at least to a certain extent, agreeing to work on behalf of the reporter and putting his or her needs above commitments to others the spokesman might have. Yes, this is frustrating, and, yes, it can even be construed as being unfair. But if done well, the payoff for the organization can be quite positive.

Reporters are like anyone else in that they gravitate to those who help make their professional lives better. Spokesman who make it a priority to be accessible to the press, even during times when not making a formal statement to the public, tend to have a more positive relationship with the press and thus are better able to exert a degree of influence over the reporters in the work they perform. This, as one would expect, has potential value to the spokesman's organization.

Framing and information subsidies are also tools for media relations practitioners that help in their agenda-influencing efforts (Zoch & Molleda, 2006). Another so-called tool that we alluded to earlier is the importance of the spokesman's ability to establish a positive working relationship with the media. Researchers have found that this adds a deeper level of agenda-setting influence on the spokesman's part. By practicing a similar approach to news value and sharing professional standards, the spokesman becomes a more active collaborator with reporters in not just what is covered but how it is covered (Berkowitz & Adams, 1990).

Persuasion

Finally, in terms of relations with the media, it is important to note that spokesman are often agents of persuasion. As a front person for any entity's public relations team, it is the spokesman who is often the driver in what public relations pioneer Edward Bernays (1923) called the *engineer of consent*. Striving to persuade, Bernays said, is what public relations professionals should and need to do on behalf of any cause, activity, or institution for which they might work. Persuasion, it should be noted, represents the attempt to shape, change, or reinforce perception and affect feelings, cognition, or behavior, particularly in regard to external publics (Pfau & Wan, 2006). Taking it a step further, one scholar even referred to persuasion and public relations as being "two 'Ps' in a pod" (Miller, 1989, p. 45). Even more bluntly, public relations is a single-minded act of advocacy (Jones, 1955). It is this mind-set the spokesman carries with him or her each and every time he or she represents the organization.

In 1984, two scholars, Grunig and Hunt, identified four public relations models in an attempt to encapsulate the diverse ways in which practitioners practiced their craft. The four models were press agentry, public information, two-way asymmetrical, and two-way symmetrical. Of the four, the primary purpose of two—press agentry and two-way asymmetrical—is to persuade targeted publics to take certain actions or adopt particular positions. Of the remaining two, the public information model is geared primarily to inform, while the purpose of the other—two-way symmetrical—is to establish a viable partnership. The insight of Grunig and Hunt served as a highlight of the importance of persuasion in acts of communication. This, of course, reinforces one of the driving goals of a spokesman each time he or she steps in front of a microphone. Via the models of Grunig and Hunt, it is highlighted that professional communicators, including spokespeople, have purposes other than persuasion in their job. Despite what many might believe, their tasks go beyond striving to generate more publicity.

They speak on behalf of their organizations or client to inform. In addition to being agents of persuasion, spokesmen are a source of information. Reporters and even members of the general public view and use them as a resource. Though surveys have indicated that public relations professionals do not necessarily see themselves in this role (Okay & Okay, 2008), to deny it as one key aspect of the spokesman's job would be to deny reality itself. Two-way symmetrical speaks to the establishment of partnerships. This, too, is part of the spokesman's job. While he or she is speaking on behalf of the organization, the spokesperson strives to do so in a way that encourages those listening to be, at the least, sympathetic to his or her perspective or, ideally, comfortable in their agreement or support of the spokesman. Granted, this is not always the easiest of challenges to face, but it remains an important element in the spokesperson's job. It also highlights how multidimensional the job of spokesman is. Each time spokesmen set out to speak to reporters or members of the public, they have multiple goals that they are attempting to meet.

This brings us back to persuasion. Persuasion underlines much of human communication (Miller & Levine, 1996). It involves an intentional effort to attempt to generate some type of cognitive, or behavioral, modification on the part of targeted audience. Thus, in keeping with this, the spokesman works to ensure that his or her efforts help maintain the client's positive image and enhance its ties to or connections with other publics. The spokesman has to balance being both a salesman and a diplomat. The long-term path to success in meeting this dual challenge must be ethical. This takes me back to an experience of mine many years before, when I was attempting to set the world on fire in little league baseball. Our team was not very good. One day after another crushing loss, our coach sat us down and told us that what is important in life it is not whether you win or lose, but rather how you play the game. A number of years had to pass before I was finally able to embrace that wisdom. It applies directly to spokesman as much as any other practitioner in communication. Not surprisingly, this captures the primary ethical challenge facing spokesmen on a day-by-day basis (Pfau & Wan, 2006). Being honest and respectful helps ensure the behavior of the entities they represent is also that way (Ewen, 2006).

Being in sync with reporters and behaving ethically helps ensure that the ties the organizational spokesman has with the media remain positive. This holds true not only in times of non-controversy but also in times of crisis when everyone is on edge and under sharper scrutiny. Behavior on the part of the organizational spokesman needs to match the level of the crisis itself. This is one of the key elements of the situational crisis communication theory, a system for matching crisis responses to crisis situations (Coombs, 2006).

Crisis Communication

My guess is that being in a serious automobile accident would be considered by many as a crisis. At the same time, winning a $100 million lottery would not be viewed in the same way. The obvious explanation for this is how the two scenarios are perceived: one negative and one positive. Yet in their examination of what constitutes a crisis, scholars have tended to put aside their judgment of the kind of unexpected turn of events that just happened and, instead, honed in on its potential ramifications. Thus, before discussing the role of the spokesman during a crisis, it is helpful to define this term, particularly as the mention of the word itself conjures images that may not necessarily be accurate. A *crisis* is a distinct moment with a potentially negative outcome that affects an organization or entity as well as its public, products, services, and reputation (Fearn-Banks, 2007). Similarly, a crisis is viewed as a potential disruption that physically affects a system as a whole and threatens its basic assumptions, its subjective sense of self, and even its existential core (Pauchart & Mitroff, 1992). A crisis possesses three defining characteristics: surprise, threat, and short response time (Hermann, 1963). Thus, the actual event or occurrence exhibiting these characteristics may actually not be negative or a so-called bad thing. (So, to those of you who one day win a multimillion-dollar lottery, keep in mind that this does not mean you are not in a crisis situation.) Depending on how it is handled or how one reacts to it in terms of behavior and attitude, it is something that could lead to significant disruption in an organization's or individual's routine. For instance, a lack of accurate information during times of uncertainty compromises an entity's ability to handle the unexpected but also potentially does harm to whatever internal morale that might have existed before a crisis (David, 2011). While the organization may have little or no control over the occurrence of a crisis, what it does largely control is its response to the crisis. This includes being able to provide accurate, adequate, timely, and coherent information to pertinent publics (David, 2011).

Experiencing crisis is as much of a reality of life as conflict itself. Even if there were such a thing as a one-person organization, that unique entity at some point would experience unwanted conflict (Starks, 2006). While seeming obvious, it is this very reality that any spokesman needs to be as well prepared for and competent in handling as he or she is at times of so-called normality. Crisis begets distress, which can and often does drag many of us down both mentally and physically (Vecchi, 2009). Of course, how well one copes with stress depends on a person's individual coping skills. As primary causes of distress include concern for physical safety and insecurities about the unknown, the organization, with the spokesman as the lead voice, can help take the steam out of these issues via open, honest, and timely messaging.

A recent example of this is found in Hurricane Sandy, the storm that rocked much of the East Coast in November 2012. Among other things, it caused millions of dollars of damage and dozens of deaths, knocked out the power in homes in multiple states, and triggered a mass exodus of residents to flee their homes and travel to parts of the country not in the storm's wake. It was a major crisis and incredibly disruptive. Government agencies and local and national media outlets collaborated to help prepare citizens for it via a range of communication efforts. While the crisis communication efforts did not lessen the impact of the storm, they did help hundreds of thousands families take the proper precautionary steps to reduce loss of life and make the anticipated disruption less stressful.

Many of us are creatures of habit. We have our routine when it comes to our day-to-day lives. When something comes along that causes us to break away from that norm, it can be a bit unsettling. Many years ago as a high school student, I packed my lunch. As a result, every day I ate a peanut butter and jelly sandwich. Partly I did this out of habit, as those tasty delights were easy to fix. But the primary reason for this routine was the fact I really enjoyed eating them. (In case you are wondering, my lunch time preference is no longer what it used to be. Today I am more of a soup-and-salad man.) In high school, I did not enjoy deviations from my regular lunch. But, on a more serious note, unexpected disruptions from our daily lives can be devastating. Losing our house and possessions in a fire is a perfect example. The result is that those who suffered the loss are feeling extremely vulnerable, ill at ease, and insecure. During times of crisis, we need stability, reassurance, and comfort. An organizational spokesman can help fill these voids via clear response strategies and a clear message (Coombs, 1999).

The reality that positive as well as negative turns of events can and do threaten the stability and well-being of an organization means that the spokesman needs to be all the more vigilant in how he or she performs his or her duties. We have seen examples of how organizations have handled unexpected situations and how that has determined their standing in the eyes of the public. I identified two notable examples of this in my own dissertation of several years ago (Walsch, 2011). One situation happened to George Mason University of Fairfax, Virginia, in March 2006, when its men's basketball team captured the imagination and interest of much the nation by defeating a number of powerhouse teams in the annual NCAA tournament and, as a result, moved all the way to coveted Final Four competition. A second example happened in February 2008 at Northern Illinois University, where a disgruntled student walked into a lecture hall and opened fire. The gunman killed five students, wounded nearly 20, and then committed suicide at the site moments before the campus police arrived to end his violent actions. In both cases the two institutions performed well in providing information to their internal and external publics at times of high scrutiny and intense, even unrelenting interest. Missteps in terms of dealing with inquiries from the media, for instance, could have unleashed false information into the public atmosphere that would in all probability have taken each institution down paths in which they would have been forced to devote time and resources to correcting false or erroneous perceptions.

Regarding the incidents in these two institutions' histories, both emerged with enhanced reputations. They were praised by peers, the media, prospective students, and the general public as being responsive to the demands placed on them in a timely and largely transparent manner. Make no mistake, being in the public spotlight means being under the public eye. In the cases of George Mason University and Northern Illinois University, each institution of higher learning represents stability within its community and region. People draw security from them. Thus, when symbols of stability such as a university are perceived to be under threat or a bit shaky, it can and often does cause uncertainty among those who utilize their services. The crisis, often unexpected, creates these feelings (Seeger, Vennette, Ulmer, & Sellnow, 2002). People generally prefer what is familiar to them. The abrupt introduction of something unfamiliar, such as in a crisis, triggers some form of outrage of those directly and indirectly affected (Sandman, 1983).

Being under the public's eye is just what it implies: the public is watching, assessing, and drawing conclusions based on what they experience, observe, and feel. Public response is both intellectual and emotional. This, then, makes the challenge of the organizational spokesman all the greater because he or she needs to speak to those two aspects of the public's psyche. The spokesman needs to balance his or her efforts to provide the public with concrete information with doing so in a way that is judged to be sensitive and sincere (Sandman & Miller, 1991). The behavior of the spokesman often influences the public's perceptions of the entity that he or she is representing. In the wake of a crisis, the public assesses the spokesman via five different components of a responsive process: (1) openness versus secrecy, (2) apology versus stonewalling, (3) courtesy versus discourtesy, (4) sharing versus confronting community values, and (5) compassion versus dispassion (Sandman, 1983). What these points speak to is not just what a spokesman says but how he or she says it. A spokesman can provide all the factually correct information, but if he or she does so in a way that is perceived to be indifferent, uncaring, flip, or begrudging, his or her comments or statements will be received in a negative light. This reminds me of the old saying: "people do not care how much you know until they know how much you care." Though it is unknown who first said it, this statement definitely applies to spokespeople. On behalf of their organizations, these communicators need to communicate that they have genuine concern for the welfare and feelings of their public. Furthermore, by communicating in an open, courteous, and caring manner, the spokesman can help keep the public's attention on the facts he or she is sharing versus how the crisis is actually being handled. So, during a crisis, it is not just the "what" but the "how" that often defines whether the spokesman has been successful or effective. For the spokesman, then, this means that his or her verbal and nonverbal messages need to be in sync throughout the duration of the crisis.

Researchers have indicated that there are several stages in the cycle of a crisis. They include pre-issue, potential, public, critical, and dormant (Crable & Vibbert, 1986). These stages speak to a public's perception of the crisis, the level of intensity of the crisis, and a consensus that the crisis has either been dealt with or contained for the foreseeable future. By properly explaining a crisis or issue, the spokesman can help the public better understand what has been or is transpiring and, therefore, be more empathetic to the organization as the crisis evolves through its stages. Just because a crisis has occurred does not mean the spokesman needs to put aside the importance of the relationship he or she has worked to develop with the public. The spokesman should never take his or her eye off that ball: maintaining a positive connection with the public and preserving the reputation of the organization. Being credible and truthful is what makes the relationship with the public, including the media, work. If anything, when public attention is heightened, a crisis provides the spokesman with a valuable opportunity to strengthen his or her ties with others. Often, public relations proves its worth in times of crisis when an organization feel surrounded by disgruntled customers and aggressive reporters (Ihlen, 2010).

Public attention—the spotlight—comes to most any organization at one time or another. Sometimes this is planned and sometimes not. Sometimes the reason for the attention rises to the level of potential disruption from the entity's routine. A crisis is one of those times when high scrutiny may not be desired, but nonetheless must be handled. Not only should the organization be properly prepared; the spokesman should be ready to play a leading role in this endeavor. Overall, the spokesman's challenge—task—is to manage issues relevant to the organization in order to minimize the chances of a crisis, seek to contain the scope of the crisis once it occurs, and lead the effort to analyze or evaluate lessons learned from the experience (Hayes, Hendrix, & Kumar, 2013). Then there is the matter of the crisis itself, particularly as it pertains to a concerned and active public. As we have discussed, it is during such a time when the spokesperson needs to (literally) step up on behalf of the organization and speak in a manner that is both open and reassuring.

But what about the period of time leading up to a crisis? Granted, a crisis, by definition, is an unexpected occurrence. Yet this is not to say that any entity or organization should not take steps to prepare for one. A classic example are the fire drills that all of us in our years as elementary school students participated in. There is no doubt that should a fire have actually occurred, while our initial reaction may have been one of surprise, thanks to the drills and professionalism and guidance of the teachers, in all likelihood our reaction would have been one of taking the proper steps to ensure our safety. Such planning speaks to risk communication, a precursor to crisis (Ihlen, 2010).

Risk communication is the process of sharing meaning about physical hazards, such as enemy attacks, plane crashes, and even fires (Rowan, 1991). Of course, risk may also be financial or moral, but traditionally it revolves around the prospect of physical threat. Though understandably and logically linked to crisis communication, there is not necessarily a role to be played by the organizational spokesman in risk communication efforts. Obviously, the spokesman needs to be well informed about steps the client or organization is taking to prepare for any unwanted, threatening circumstance. The spokesman can do this by playing a prominent role in the organization's crisis management team. Serving on such a team helps ensure a healthy linkage between the entity's risk and crisis communication plans. But this does not necessarily mean that the spokesman needs to be one of the communication professionals who has a hands-on role in the preparation and dissemination of materials and communiqués designed to inform or educate employees about potential crises.

Just as preparing and executing promotional strategies requires the active involvement of the spokesman, so, too, do those efforts to help contend with matters when a crisis occurs. This speaks to *crisis management*, the process designed to prevent or lessen the damage a crisis can inflict on an organization and its stakeholders (Coombs, 2007). Crisis management speaks to all three aspects of an unwanted situation: preparation, actual response, and assessment. By the nature of his or her role in communicating to the entity's publics, the spokesman needs to be a key member of this team. Organizational members, particularly the spokesman, must be prepared to talk with the media during a crisis (Lerbinger, 1997). Of course, in today's world with more technological options at the fingertips of communicators than ever before, communicating with the public can and should involve more than simply having a spokesman make himself or herself available to questions from the press (though this is important). Websites with timely information can be crafted. Having key players within an organization speak to their staff is another option (Taylor & Kent, 2007). Even establishing hotlines to which members of the public can call with questions and updates is a viable consideration. Collectively, they represent elements of a comprehensive strategy to keep the public and other interested elements in the loop on what is transpiring. Again, the spokesman needs to be kept informed of each of these communication efforts.

In terms of communication, all three of these phases of a crisis are important to an organization's reputation and image. If not handled well, there is little doubt that the entity can suffer harm that could have an uncomfortably long shelf life. Of the phases, however, the most critical for the spokesman is in the response to it while it is ongoing. During this time, not only has the dust not settled; it is still stirring, without a clear clue as to where it will eventually land. For the spokesman, the guidelines as to steps he or she must take are clear. What he or she says must be quick, accurate, and consistent (Coombs, 2007). Let there be no misunderstanding here: none of this is easy. A serious miscue on the spokesman's part can have long-term ramifications for him or her, for those involved in the crisis, and for the organization. This is why crisis communication must be viewed as a major component of the spokesman's job, despite the fact a crisis is a rare occurrence.

Something terrible happens, and people immediately want to know what is going on and how it affects them. A quick response by the organization demonstrates that it is in control of the situation (Carney & Jorden, 1993). Silence, regardless of the reasons for it, is generally interpreted by the public in a negative way. They tend to view the organization as being passive, possibly trying to sweep information under the rug or not caring (Hearit, 1994). In addition, a slow response also makes it possible for others—namely the media—to take greater control of how the story is presented to the public. Once such a loss of control occurs, the organization, through the spokesman, is positioned into being more reactive to how others perceive what has been or is transpiring.

Obviously, providing the public with accurate information is extremely important. At the same time, gathering information and confirming its validity takes time. But often during a crisis, such as a massive fire or shootings, time is not always on the side of the ones who are doing the communicating. Not all of the pertinent facts are known, yet people want information right away. They have questions they want answered now. Plus, there may be a circumstance where people may be at risk. What the public needs here is what Sturges called *instructing information* (1994). What does the organization do? What advice can and should the spokesman give to help with this dilemma? The answer is found in not letting the public, and this includes the media, wait. Even telling people "We do not yet know" is better than saying nothing at all. It is acceptable to come forward with partial information, so long as the spokesman is upfront about this. Tell reporters what you know to be true. If questions are put forth that you either do not know the answer to or have not been able to confirm, it is acceptable to say, "I do not know, but I will get back to you on this." This is why, particularly if a story is unfolding, communicators schedule press briefings during a crisis situation on an ongoing basis, such as every hour. Doing so reassures an anxious public that efforts are being made to collect and share new information as quickly as possible. As we have already suggested, the more information people have, the less anxiety they tend to feel, and the less likely it is their confidence in the organization will erode.

Particularly during a crisis, one would be hard-pressed to find any professional communicators who believe organizations should be represented by multiple spokespeople. Researchers support this. The philosophy of speaking with one voice in a crisis is a way of maintaining accuracy (Coombs, 2007). However, Coombs adds, "This does not mean only one person speaks for the organization for the duration of the crisis" (p. 6). From a practical perspective, it is physically impossible for one person to do all the speaking, especially if the crisis goes beyond even one day (Barton, 2001). This is why is it paramount that those designated to speak on a particular issue need to be briefed briefly thoroughly to ensure that what they say is in harmony. The last thing multiple spokespeople want is to contradict each other. The key here is the information. The specific spokesman, though vital, at best runs a close second to what is shared with the public.

A good illustration of a crisis handled well as a result of a well-coordinated communication effort on the part of the organization and its lead communicators, including the spokesman, is an incident involving the U.S. Department of Agriculture and the National Cattleman's Beef Association in 2003. A cow in Washington state was diagnosed with bovine spongiform encephalopathy, or mad cow disease, a fatal neurodegenerative disease transferrable to humans. This was of great concern, as even a single case had been known to be quite destructive in other countries such as the United Kingdom, Germany, and Canada. A proactive and unified communication effort was launched immediately (Hendrix & Hayes, 2007). Working together and utilizing one unified voice/message, the Department of Agriculture and beef industry targeted national and international press, along with various beef councils and cattlemen's associations, to squelch unfounded rumors from gaining traction as well as inaccurate information from being disseminated. The results were quite positive: beef demand increased, and consumer confidence remained strong. In addition, the public became better informed about mad cow disease. These results did not happen in other countries, as their response was tepid.

Chapter Highlights

- The organizational spokesman needs to be as concerned with internal relations as he or she is with external relations.
- The spokesman should have a good working relationship with all segments of the organization.
- When it comes to external relations, the general public should be just as important to the spokesman as the media is.
- Framing, information subsidies, and agenda setting provide a good road map in helping spokesmen control their messages to external audiences.
- Persuasion is a key element of any message or statements put forth by a spokesman.
- All spokesmen should have a clearly defined crisis communication plan to follow.

Discussion Questions

- What would be effective strategies for spokesmen to follow to establish a good working relationship with the organization's internal publics?
- Why is framing a message important?
- Discuss the pros and cons of going "off the record" with members of the media.
- Where do you believe the spokesman belongs on an entity's organizational chart?
- What should be the key communication components of a spokesman during a crisis?

FOCUS ON

Howard Opinsky, Executive Vice President of Hill-Knowlton Strategies, and General Manager of the Firm's Washington, D.C., Office

Opinsky focuses on corporate and public affairs client engagements and driving growth, enhancing client service, and managing business operations. He brings a combination of experience from politics, consulting, and the highest levels of major global corporations to the firm and its clients. A veteran communications strategist and spokesperson, Opinsky was most recently managing director of global corporate communications at JP Morgan Chase & Company. While there, Opinsky led communications about corporate performance, operations, and corporate responsibility activities, as well as conducted public affairs work to address legislative and regulatory issues that impacted the firm.

His numerous clients have included Bank of America, Cisco Systems, Mattel, Microsoft, Northrop Grumman, Siemens, the U.S. Chamber of Commerce, Business Roundtable, and the governments of the United States and Colombia. In addition, he has served as a political communication strategist and spokesman for local, state, and national political campaigns. Opinsky holds a bachelor of arts in political communication from The George Washington University.

Question: What led you to a career in communication?

Answer: In college, I studied political communication and became fascinated by the interaction between information and what I call the publication of that information. As I learned more about it, I came to realize that many journalists were getting their information from someone else. I felt it would be great to learn more about that "someone else." Perhaps even become that person.

I started becoming more involved in politics as I gained my own perspective on things. I saw the crafting of communication as an important challenge and quickly realized there was a career in that field.

It was back in high school where I had my first real taste of communication. I was not on the high school newspaper, but I had a great internship at the St. Louis Post-Dispatch that really set me on my path. I spent time looking at different parts of the paper and was able to spend some time working in their Washington bureau. I even was able to sit in on a one-on-one interview with Congressman Dick Gebhardt of Missouri just before he announced his plan to run for president. That was exciting.

In college, I had another great internship at a local television station. Watching these broadcast professionals gather news, put it together, and then communicate it to the public helped me get interested in the mechanics of information sharing, politics, and governance—how that gathering intersects with the sharing and interpretation of it.

Question: Do you see your role of spokesman as being one of advocacy or education? Are you an advocate, an educator, or both?

Answer: Oftentimes both. I have never been in the role of having to be an unbiased spokesman for an agency or client. All my spokesman roles have been representing someone who has a point of view. Without question, one has to balance being an advocate with being informative and keeping people's attention. The trick in doing this is being credible—being part of an honest dialogue. You need to put forth your point of view not blindly but with a cogent argument. Facts are facts and cannot and should not be denied.

Everyone has a point of view, and that's fine. But being a good spokesman is having a strong command of your facts. Being factual is the best way to maintain credibility. People may not always agree with you, but by being honest and accurate with the information you share, they are more apt to listen and not simply tune you out.

Establishing a good command of the fact requires a lot of work. I tell people there is more to being a spokesman than simply standing in front of a microphone and talking. It requires a great deal of research and preparation.

Question: What skill set should a spokesman possess?

Answer: One has to be intellectually curious. A person should be inquisitive. They need to be willing to take the time to study issues. They should be strategically minded, [and] have a good sense of how things will be received. This involves knowing about the people to whom you are speaking: stakeholders, the media, and the general public. Also, it is important to be a good writer. I say that because good writers are able to organize their thoughts well. This is one thing spokesmen need to do.

Another key aspect is being credible within your organization. Part of this means being fearless with your client. In coming up with message points, either for yourself or the person you are representing, you need to raise the tough questions—the ones no one wants to answer. It may turn out you are the one who has to answer them, so in your planning sessions this helps you and the others prepare. Asking those tough questions comes from having a good idea of what you might be asked. It also requires being tenacious. Don't let people put you off from being the one who raises those difficult or uncomfortable questions. It may be awkward, but it is better for everyone.

Question: Generally, what are some pitfalls a spokesman might run into?

Answer: The most important thing is to not lie. If people don't recognize the lie right away, they soon will. It's fine to have a particular point of view, but not your own set of facts. Facts are the truth, and that's what you must work from.

The spokesman is a convenient trip of the spear. Issues arise, and a person is needed to speak to them, is needed to answer questions about them. That is you. At the same time, oftentimes while you may have a good idea on what to say, you still need to gather internal support of those talking points. Sometimes just getting the approval of your primary client is not enough. You will need to get other advisors or key members of the organization behind you as well. This helps reduce being second-guessed or undermined by others. One potential problem is when the spokesman does not get as much internal support as they should or need.

Another pitfall is lacking message discipline. It's amazing how often people stray from their original message or even speak with no regard for the facts. In today's world, people fact-check constantly. So, if you are loose with the facts or don't pay attention to them, then you will be caught pretty quickly. This affects your credibility. When you speak to others, you need to have a mission, know what it is you are going to say. Know why you are speaking.

I think most people can pick out a good spokesman from one that is not so good. Sometimes people get lost in their words. They begin talking and somewhere along the way stop making sense, particularly in a live interview. Spokesman fail when they do not have a good grasp of the facts, when they do not have the ability to answer basic questions.

Question: How would you describe the role of the spokesman?

Answer: There is a functional purpose for this person. They are present to respond to inquiries in a timely and professional way. Also, ideally they need to be part of the decision making that goes into deciding what is to be communicated. There are those who serve strictly as a mouthpiece. This is fine, but as they establish their internal credibility, they can play a greater role in helping determine what to say—how best to respond to the public. Also, the spokesman's role is to be a bridge between who you represent and the stakeholders and the media. At times, this involves simply providing basic information without any kind of explanation. We all do this, especially those who are starting out as spokesmen.

Finally, a spokesman should never forget that a person's reputation is often impacted by how they are perceived. As the spokesman becomes more visible, oftentimes how the public sees the spokesman is how they see the client.

Source: H. Opinsky (personal communication, February, 2012).

Chapter Three

Measuring Success and Effectiveness

From time to time, one of the most fundamental questions any of us ask ourselves as it relates to our jobs, our relationships, our lives, and any other aspect of our being is, "How am I doing?" This is a very basic question, yet one that is not always easy to answer. None of us, in this regard, is like a sports team in that we simply have to look up at the scoreboard to see who has scored the most runs or accumulated the most points. When sports teams ask the question, the answer is straightforward.

For those of us who do not live lives in those kind of athletic situations, that fundamental question is a lot trickier—not nearly so straightforward. This is certainly the case for organizational spokesmen. What defines the answer to that question for them is found in a much more gray context. Much of the wellness of their efforts is found in the world of relationships, perceptions, interactions, and bias. In the context of each of these components, rarely are things all good or all bad, all success or all failure, all smooth or all rough. That reality, one might conclude, is what makes the job of spokesman not always as gratifying or satisfying as one might like. This is, in fact, one reason why some communicators do not want to step into this kind of role. (By the same token, the challenge of fulfilling such a murky role is one reason why some actually do.) Either way, such is the world in which the organizational spokesman dwells.

As the spokesman, this professional is the out-front person. His or her actions and words play a key role in helping shape how publics relate to an organization. At the same time, they are not marketers or even publicists in the classic sense of the words, so spokesmen cannot be held directly accountable for ticket sales to an event, for example, membership drives, or raising a profit margin. Other communicators play a more direct role in those and other related efforts. The spokesman is in the unique position of being both a leading advocate for increased sales or profits though not the communicator who directs or even instigates campaigns designed to achieve those goals. Despite this, it is not uncommon for the spokesman to be viewed as the one whose actions determine a campaign's success, primarily because he or she plays such a visible role on behalf of the organization and all that it does and seeks to attain.

Given that, the basic question remains: how does the spokesman determine his or her success? When this communicator goes home at the end of a workday and reflects on what transpired, what criteria does he or she use to judge whether the day has been a good one? Before delving into the specifics of this, it is important to outline the evolution of this bottom-line question from a broad perspective. Measuring the success of any public relations effort has long been a point of discussion and even debate among public relations practitioners. Traditionally, when it comes to return on investment (ROI), the standard definition has been the amount of income earned through public relations initiatives after subtracting program expenditures. However, when it comes to public relations, many view this as not necessarily being the best measure (Rockland, 2005). Furthermore, according to surveys, the great majority of professional communicators agree that measurement of their efforts is important even though there remains little understanding or agreement as to the best or most appropriate ways to design and implement an effective system of design and measurement (Michaelson & Macleod, 2007). Even the notion of scientific measuring efforts has not always been embraced by practitioners.

As far back as 1983, communication scholar James Grunig observed that many public relations practitioners paid lip service to the importance of measurement. The following year, he and others said that, while acknowledging the value of measurement and concrete assessment, many in the profession seemed content to "fly by the seat of their pants" (Grunig & Hunt, 1984). Though these early misgivings eventually evolved toward greater acknowledgement that, yes, measurement is important, there remained—and still remains—an attitude among some that measurement and evaluation need be more anecdotal and informal (Macnamara, 2005) rather than statistics-driven. At the same time, other scholars have moved forward with specific proposals on ways in which public relations professionals can better measure their efforts and ways in which their organizational superiors can measure them as well. One model of measurement that can be applied to organizational spokesman was designed by Cutlip, Center, and Broom (1985). It is called a PII model. In it, three primary criteria—impact, implementation, and preparation—are the benchmarks by which communication efforts are measured.

In the area of impact, the question of what changes in attitude and/or behavior on a public's part have been made as a result of communication strategies are focused on. Regarding implementation, such matters as who attends to messaging and how many messages are distributed to the public are weighed. Finally, in regard to preparation, the content of the message and the quality of its presentation are assessed. Using these as guidelines, it is easy to see how the efforts of an organizational spokesman could be inserted into such a matrix. The spokesman is a key component in the distribution of messages and efforts to elicit support or approval from the public. In attempting to achieve such ends, it can be seen how the person in front of the microphone or on the receiving end of questions from reporters must deliver messages that are clear, timely and information-driven. As part of the measuring effort, this professional's impact—if any—on the public's attitude can also be a factor in any assessment of his or her work.

Formal research does not readily apply itself to the efforts of the organizational spokesman. The spokesman dwells more in a world of nuance, attitude, perceptions, and timing rather than hard numbers and statistics. A quick review of the basic steps included in a formal research effort reinforces this. These steps include stating the problem one wishes to address; developing a hypothesis; designing experiments to test the hypothesis; obtaining, analyzing, and interpreting data; and then communicating the results. While I am not suggesting that hard data cannot be gleaned from a formal assessment of the spokesman's work, if such an effort were to be made, it makes more sense to include this data in the context of an examination of the organization's overall public relations or communication effort. The spokesman role, as we have already indicated, is one part of that mix.

Even using the criteria one finds in formal research efforts does not necessarily result in hard data, however. Furthermore, the spokesman, though highly and obviously visible, is not the only player in a comprehensive strategy. What the spokesman does is often designed to complement a range of other strategies, including communiqués to the media, information on an organization's web page, announcements sent out via such social media outlets as Twitter and Facebook, paid advertisements, and interviews with highly ranked officials within the entity. Collectively, these strategies are the primary focus of any comprehensive assessment effort. Evaluating the performance of the spokesman consists of a combination of what I term aesthetics and observation. Neither one of these lends itself to statistics or other hard data—or, at least, does so without taking into account other parts of a comprehensive strategic communication plan. This, then, is a difference between the organizational spokesman and a more traditional public relations practitioner who is often judged on the basis of such things as earned media or direct mail returns.

Because of the uniqueness of the position of spokesman, additional factors need to be identified when it comes to measurement. As the spokesman, by definition, is the organization's point person—the one often out front of the entity's outreach—how the spokesman is evaluated should revolve around how well he or she, in a sense, clears the weeds between the client and the targeted publics. An advantage to being that out-front person is that one is the first to experience and/or witness public reaction to the communiqués put forth. The initial reactions are directed as the conveying of those messages. Thus, being on the receiving end gives them a unique perspective on their organization's communication effort and its effectiveness. Granted, their assessment as to what they see and/or hear initially may not be scientific, but it remains helpful in any organization's analysis of its communication efforts. Being in such an advantageous position to monitor early reactions—good or bad—is one more reason why the spokesman is such a vital player in the public relations process. As a result, in this regard, I speak of what can be construed as traditional categories of communication barriers and how well they are overcome. Following are categories of communication barriers that are addressed on a regular basis by any organizational spokesman: nature of the audience, audience attitude, opposition or competition, exposure, and nature of the media. Each of these categories represents barriers if communicators misread and misinterpret the information that each implies or imparts.

Nature of the Audience

Every audience or public is diverse. Even if the group is comprised of people of the same race or religion, it remains comprised of men and women of varying socioeconomic backgrounds, interests, biases, and so forth. The result is people with different experiences and backgrounds. According to the 2012 United States Census Bureau, the country's total population is approximately 315 million people. Of those, 155 million are female, and the remaining are male. The great majority of Americans (82%) live either in a city or the suburbs and an equally large majority (77%) consider themselves to be white. The U.S. population is highly diverse. As projected by the Census Bureau, in the coming decades its diversity is only going to grow. For communicators, this means greater challenges in devising strategies that will also need to be more diverse (pardon the pun) or multidimensional.

With this diversity, the need for the professional communicators, including the spokesman, to target messages or communiqués in ways that speak to the needs and interests of specific publics increases. In a nation as diverse as the United States, communication as a one-size-fits-all enterprise is not nearly what it used to be. This is particularly true in these times of technological advancement, when outreach efforts can be better fine-tuned to specific ears. Interestingly, however, this reality does not always apply to the spokesman. Oftentimes this professional finds himself or herself talking to the general public in interactions with representatives of the mainstream media. In those scenarios, spokesmen are not always able to couch their comments in ways that speak to specific sections of the population. Thus, even though they may recognize the diversity of the general public and are sensitive to the traits of each segment, in making their comments, spokesmen focus on sharing information that speaks primarily to the common needs and/or interests of each segment. In this case, the spokesman is not like the public relations professional who is in a better position to target specific messages to specific audiences or publics.

It is ironic, then, that the general duties of the spokesman tend to make him or her not as well positioned to advance an organization's strategies as some of its other communicators might be. Spokesmen are not as able to tap directly into the various aspects that comprise the nature of the audience as they and their organizations' superiors might prefer or even assume they do. Still, this is not to say that they cannot help manage their entities' public relations efforts by seeking to control publics, respond to publics, or establish mutually beneficial relations with publics (Newsom, Turk, & Kruckeberg, 2013). As we have covered, spokesmen can and do affect public perceptions based as much on the level of their performance as the information they share.

Audience Attitude

Without question, even the most open-minded have preconceptions of numerous issues and topics. Each of us draws from the array of experiences—good and bad—that we collect over our years. Collectively, they help shape our thinking, mold our preferences, and serve as internal gatekeepers as to which information and sources of information we are more receptive to. All this is to say that we carry around with us attitudes. While some of these feelings have a longer shelf life than others, they determine our level of receptivity to messages and information shared with us. For instance, a person may have strong feelings regarding capital punishment. Let us say this person supports it. If that person finds himself or herself being talked at by another who is against it, his or her level of attention may be low. On the other hand, if the person finds himself or herself in conversation with someone who shares this view, his or her attitude is likely to be one of closer attention. This simple example illustrates the role the attitude of an audience or public likely plays in the effectiveness of messages directed toward them. If the sender of that message, such as an organization's spokesman, is aware of that attitude, he or she might try framing that message in a way that speaks directly to the attitude. For instance, one tactic is to openly acknowledge an audience's skepticism toward a given topic and then put forth points that speak to it while giving them opportunities to voice their concerns or raise questions.

Speaking to an audience with a questioning, skeptical, hostile, or even apathetic attitude brings to mind what has come to be called "The Press Secretary's Prayer": "Oh, Lord, let me utter words sweet and gentle, for tomorrow, I may have to eat them" (, . Uttered by one of President Ronald Reagan's deputy press secretaries, Pete Roussel (2006), the quote reflects the uncertainty press secretaries often carry with them when stepping in front of an audience they anticipate is present to do more than listen. They are present to challenge or possibly refute. This can be a tough gig, as someone in show business might say. Nevertheless, the spokesman must face the audience's attitude in a manner that best reflects that which he or she is representing and the information or message he or she is imparting. The spokesman's attitude must be professional, positive, respectful, and firm, even during times when the audience's attitude may not be any of those things.

Opposition or Competition

More often than not, no matter how well we are saying something, there is always someone else who is voicing or putting forth a competing message that provides publics with an alternative prospective. Political advertisements provide a wealth of examples of this. On television, for example, a commercial may be run by a candidate outlining why he or she is the best qualified to win the election. The next commercial break may find an equally impressive advertisement being aired by that person's opponent making an equally convincing case as to why he or she should be elected. Of course, this does not just happen during election seasons. We see competition between various products and even charities. For the public, of course, it can be a dilemma as to which one to listen to or support. For those doing the messaging, it is a tougher dilemma, as they have the challenge of being even more convincing than their competitors while being respectful, accurate, and fair. This, of course, is not in any way meant to be an indirect criticism of this kind of scenario, as competition represents the essence of our free-enterprise system. Much like a 100-yard dash between two or more athletes, there are often winners and losers. The risk of being a loser at any given time is a communication barrier and one that the spokesman faces with much regularity.

Exposure

Another tricky challenge faced by the spokesman is gaining the proper amount of exposure so that his or her message and corresponding information will be properly heard and understood. As is the case with each of these communication barriers, there is no guarantee that these obstacles will be overcome as thoroughly as might be hoped. Life being what it is, so much goes on in the world and in people's individual lives that competes for a person's attention. All of this potentially serves as a deterrent to preventing the spokesman's message from gaining the attention or exposure it often needs. It is because of this reality, of course, that so many strategic communication plans are comprised of more than one tactic in an effort to promote a product or image. As important as the spokesman is in this process, he or she is not the only part of the overall plan. That, in no way, should be interpreted as a weakness on the spokesman's part or on the position itself. All effective communication plans are comprehensive in terms of tactics that are utilized and publics that are targeted. The spokesman cannot and should not be expected to be able to achieve all of an organization's communication goals.

What can the spokesman do to help ensure that his or her message receives as much attention as the spokesman and the client or organization wishes? Realistically, not a whole lot. However, by being straightforward, articulate, transparent, and empathetic to the wishes of others, the spokesman can contribute to the client's outreach efforts. It is a matter of going back to the cliché about being part of the solution or the problem. By doing his or her job well, the spokesman can be a tangible benefit to any entity.

Nature of the Media

All people carry around with them information of some sort. Granted, some may have a broader base of knowledge than others, but no one's head is totally devoid of information (even though it may sometimes seem like it). The other piece of that equation is that information had to come from somewhere. It had a source. The challenge for any public relations professional wishing to connect with a targeted public is to identify the specific sources of information to which they turn to obtain information. For instance, senior citizens may utilize the magazine produced regularly by the American Association of Retired Persons (AARP) as a source of information. They would be far less inclined to tap into various social media outlets or a publication geared toward much younger readers such as *Us Weekly*. With that knowledge, the organization and its communicators, including the spokesman when appropriate, can gear their communiqués to match the vehicle with its likely reader or viewership.

Once that is done, it is a matter of trying to send information through those channels in order to reach those targeted publics. Popular ways to do this include press releases, paid advertisements, public service announcements, calendars, and successfully pitching stories. The trick is to successfully match information that is of greatest interest to a specific public with the communication vehicle or vehicles on which they rely for information.

Also, the spokesman can help in this regard by making himself or herself available to reporters from individual newspapers or news outlets, for instance. It is not uncommon for politicians to grant these type of exclusive interviews to correspondents from individual television or radio stations or reporters from various print outlets. Such actions help meet the journalistic needs of the media, develop a level of goodwill, and help ensure stories or information that the organization's representative is trying to get out will receive the desired coverage.

Overcoming Barriers

The nature of the audience, audience attitude, opposition or competition, exposure, and the nature of the media represent barriers if the communicator misuses or misinterprets the information that each represents. The best strategy for ensuring that these categories do not become barriers is for the communicator to get to know his or her targeted publics as thoroughly as possible. There is no substitute for this. Nothing can replace having a wide and deep knowledge base about publics with which the organization has a relationship with or hopes to. With this information, the entity is better able to time its communiqués properly, set the proper wording and tone for them, disseminate them with greater accuracy, and, thus, be more successful in its outreach efforts.

As the spokesman is one part of the communication process, this professional cannot and should not be expected to overcome all potential or real barriers being faced by an organization. He or she is the one who, metaphorically, highlights the key points in the organization's press releases, emphasizes the priorities of the entity that have been set forth by the chief executive officer to stakeholders, and helps address any concerns or questions the public might have. The spokesman is the explainer, the one who reassures, the comforter, and the carrier of difficult or even happy news. Thus, the spokesman is often the one who first receives the initial reaction to what is announced. It is hard to attach data to this unique role and measure the spokesman's efforts in what would be considered traditional ways. This is not to imply that the spokesman is beyond assessment or review. What I do suggest is that any evaluation of this person should be far more attitudinal than statistical, or a balanced combination of the two. This can be a double-edged sword. Assessment of the work of the spokesman is more subjective than objective. Those doing the judging often do so more based on feelings and anecdotal observation or feedback than actual data. As a result, any time this is the case, when emotions and intellect are not equal partners, there is often greater room for an interpretative critique. Depending on one's perspective or vantage point, this can be either positive or negative. Thus, review time for the spokesman can be more of a nail-biting experience than it is for most others. With luck, those doing the assessing will have enough of a communication background to help ensure that their critique is even-handed.

Rules to Work By

As is the case with any job or in any profession, there are a number of dos and don'ts when it comes to working as a spokesman that help determine the success or competence of such a professional. The bulk of these, I should note, are derived from my own experience working with press secretaries or spokesmen and serving as one myself. While I do not pretend this to be a definitive list, it is hopefully substantive enough to give one a strong sense of the behavior that is expected of these professionals by their peers, colleagues, and organizational superiors. Also, though some of the items on the list may seem to be a simple matter of common sense, that does not make them any less valid or notable.

Dos

- Remain loyal to your organization. You are its representative.
- Respect reporters and their work. They, like you, are communicators attempting to connect with the public.
- Stick to your message or talking points.
- Keep trying to be the best communicator you can be.
- The best way to look on camera is believable. For the spokesperson, that is far better than being "pretty" or "handsome."
- Remember that you are in the relationship business. This means that your job is to help build and maintain bridges between your organization and its publics. This also means that part of your job is to conduct yourself in a manner that demonstrates your concern for the welfare of the public, particularly those with whom your organization or client partners.
- Keep your commitments.
- Be accessible, even when it is not convenient.
- Be an active member of your organization's communication team.
- Remember that while being articulate is important, being honest is better.
- Dress professionally.
- Be punctual.
- Be timely.
- Cut yourself and others some slack. No one communicates perfectly all the time—not you or anyone else.
- Do all you can to complement the words and action of your organization's leader. Your job is to support, not compete.

Don'ts

- Do not ignore questions asked of you, even if your response is "I do not know" or "I cannot or will not respond to that question at this time."
- Do not allow yourself to be isolated from all elements of your organization.
- Do not forget that you are a receiver as well as a sender of messages and information.
- Do you not let your guard down when talking with reporters. Everything you say can and will be used in a story.

- Do not shortchange research. The more you know about a topic, the better you are able to speak about it.
- Do not forget that people often judge your organization or client based on how they assess you.
- Do not choose informality over formality. This applies to dress, interaction with others, and demeanor.
- Do not lose your sense of humor. It is always a good companion.
- Do not take yourself too seriously. You may be articulate, and you may appear in the news frequently, but do not take that lightly or ever forget much always rides on how well prepared you are and how well you do.
- Do not mislead. It is just as dishonest as lying.
- Do not lose sight of the fact that even though you are a communication leader, you are also part of a team.
- Do not confuse perfection with being understood.
- Your job is not about you. It is about representing others. Do not confuse the two.
- Do not represent an organization or cause you do not believe in. Life is too short to go to bat for something you have little or no regard for.
- In the communication business, you do not put off until tomorrow what you can and should do today.

Chapter Highlights

- Measuring the success of the spokesman is not as straightforward as measuring the success of other public relations practitioners.
- The spokesman can play a key role in helping an organization or client overcome traditional communication barriers.
- Five categories of primary communication barriers include the nature of the media, the nature of the audience, audience attitude, opposition or competition, and exposure. The best way to overcome them is to know as much about your audience or targeted public as possible.
- Duties performed by the spokesman serve as a key component in the overall communication process.

Discussion Questions

- What do you believe are the best ways to evaluate the performance of a spokesman?
- Should the spokesman be assessed by the same criteria used to evaluate an organization's press agent or public relations director?
- Describe the manner in which a spokesman should conduct himself or herself when on the job. Are there any differences between the spokesman's behavior and that of other public relations practitioners?

FOCUS ON

Nancy Mitchell Pfotenhauer, President of the Communications Firm MediaSpeak Strategies

Prior to launching her company, Nancy Mitchell Pfotenhauer served as a senior policy advisor and national spokesman for the McCain for President campaign, appearing almost daily on cable networks. She is the former president and CEO of the Independent Women's Forum (IWF), serving in that position from 2000 to 2005. She was vice chairman of IWF's Board of Directors from 2005 to 2007.

A veteran television and radio commentator, Pfotenhauer has gained a national reputation for being able to reduce difficult public policy issues to lively, easily understood, and memorable subject of discourse for television, cable, and radio audiences. As a daily morning talk show host for NET, she made the case for free market policy solutions to problems facing the country. Her television and cable appearances include segments on NBC, ABC, CNN, MSNBC, FOX, and PBS. She has appeared on the cover of *National Journal* and been featured in *Newsweek, The Washington Post, The Wall Street Journal*, and *The Washington Times*.

Pfotenhauer began her career in Washington, D.C., in 1987 as a senior economist at the Republican National Committee. The following year she was promoted to senior economist. In 1990, she joined the president's council on regulatory review group. This appointment involved daily interaction with the highest-level career and political personnel at the Office of Management and Budget, the Environmental Protection Agency, and the U.S. Departments of Agriculture, Energy, the Interior, Transportation, and the Treasury. In addition, she has served as a delegate to the United Nation's Commission on the Status of Women, a member of the National Advisory Committee on Violence Against Women, and various advisory committees to the secretaries of labor and energy.

Pfotenhauer holds a bachelor's degree in economics from the University of Georgia and a master of arts degree in economics from George Mason University. She currently serves as vice rector of the institution's Board of Visitors.

Question: A very fundamental question might be a good place to start. What is the purpose of an organizational spokesman?

Answer: Such a person provides a client or organization with a qualified voice. They help give people a sense of familiarity with an organization, help give them a fix on the organization. It is not unlike a familiar logo or character of some sort. People see a familiar face and hopefully think of the organization in a positive way. So, you could say there is a marketing element tied to being a spokesman.

Consumers today gather their information and news in so many different ways. They are multitasking and no longer relying necessarily on one newspaper or one television station for their information. The spokesman gives them a continuity—a common thread—with all those sources.

Question: Is there a particular set of skills one should have to become an effective spokesman?

Answer: Being a spokesman—a good one—is hard work. Such a person needs to have an analytical ability and a willingness to do a lot of research on any given subject. Even if you are the designated spokesman, it is you and no one else in front of that camera. You are doing the talking. You are answering the questions. You must be extremely well versed on a topic, know the audience to whom you are speaking, and have a good understanding of the opportunity you have when in front of a camera as well as the threat. As best you can, you must be able to anticipate the questions a reporter is going to ask and, if you are on camera with another spokesman representing an opposing side, know what their perspectives are so you can [speak] to them more easily. Try to develop a good understanding of what it is your opponent is going to say. This involves strategic thinking.

Question: As a spokesman, is your purpose to advocate or educate or both?

Answer: This depends on the topic. You try to educate as you advocate. If you have done your homework well, you should be able to speak to the topic with confidence. Your research should identify what I call knowledge gaps that you can try to fill by working closely with your client. Know your media. Know your audience. Don't make assumptions on what they know or understand. So, as you respond to questions, you may have to try and educate but not in a way that is condescending or too simple.

Question: How does one build or maintain bridges with a public that may be hostile to our position?

Answer: If you are in an openly hostile environment, do not take the bait and be hostile back at the interviewer or reporter. Nasty does not dial well. People do not enjoy listening to two people shout at each other or talk over each other. It is the style of some interviewers to get their guest riled up. Do not take that bait, as tempting as it may be.

In this regard, something else a spokesman should not try to do it litigate a point. Don't go into the weeds on a topic. It is possible you may know more than your opponent or the reporter, but if you start using technical terms or jargon, you are very likely to lose your audience. Don't fall into the inside baseball trap. I cannot emphasize enough the importance of being prepared. This includes knowing the public you are trying to reach and the best way to talk to them. You must know your universe every time you step into an interview situation. You have one shot to fire, so be prepared.

Question: You have alluded several times to being strategic. Can you talk a bit more about that?

Answer: This goes back to being as thoroughly prepared as you can as well as working closely with your client. When working as a spokesman, one goes from being a mouthpiece to a strategic partner. Before sitting down in front of a camera or microphone, sit down with your client and discuss the topic, questions you anticipate being asked, and answers to them you feel should be given. Part of this internal process involves taking on the role of reporter and asking your client hard questions you anticipate being asked. Just know, if you are going to play the reporter and do it well, then you must be thoroughly prepared. Interview situations must be taken seriously. Are you stepping into a hostile situation? Are you trying to persuade, or is your audience generally friendly and open to your message?

Career-wise, it takes a while to get to the point where you are able to sit down with the politician or CEO you are representing, ask them tough questions, and then help them articulate effective responses that are understandable. Sitting down with the client at these times is a challenge-process. You are there to challenge them but hopefully have the credibility and trust so they know you are doing this to benefit them and what they represent. It is important to remember as a spokesman you are never the puppet. You are an active, strategic partner.

Of course, depending upon the situation, sometimes you are not the best person to be out front. If it's good news, then who wouldn't want the CEO out there talking about it? But if it is not or if it's a crisis situation, then no doubt you are working with a team of folks, some of whom may be in a better position to be the voice or face because of their expertise.

Question: Your background is in economics. What path did you take to becoming a media strategist and spokesman?

Answer: Economics is a method of analysis. This plays well into the strategic thinking that goes with being a successful spokesman. Economists have certain way of talking. So do lawyers. Spokesman have a way of framing things, too. In communication, you have to communicate clearly but quickly. I was thrown into the deep end and was able to swim. I have learned that being glib or being pretty or handsome is not enough. Nor should one ever confuse being lucky with being good. Preparation is the key. People with designs on becoming a spokesman need to learn their craft. They need to be able to think very quickly on their feet and have a tremendous information process and retrieval skill set. It is not unlike watching an athlete. The spokesman is performing in real time. You always have to be thinking, making instant judgment calls, yet do so in a way that is understandable.

As it pertains to being part of an organization, your job is to know what the company or client does, of course. But mainly you should follow the clips. Know what the public's knowledge is. Your focus should be more on what is happening and being discussed externally.

Being a spokesman is one of those professions that people feel they can do better than you. You get second-guessed a lot. But what you are doing is very important and central to any overall communication effort.

Source: N. M. Pfotenhauer (personal communication, January, 2013).

Chapter Four

Legal and Ethical Aspects

Let me begin this chapter by stating the obvious: no one is above the law. This includes press secretaries or organizational spokespeople. They can be sent off to "the big house" as easily as anyone who breaks the law. Thus, any notion that they are immune to legal actions should be tossed out the window right now. The question is, in their capacity as a spokesmen, what do they have to do for that unwanted scenario to happen? At the same time, where and how do professional ethics fit into performing the duties of this communication job? For communicators, acting within the law and conducting oneself in an ethical manner fall under the larger umbrella of maintaining one's credibility. If there is one thing lawbreakers and those found to behave unethically have in common, is that neither has much, if any, credibility. One overall purpose of this chapter is to focus on what spokespeople need to do to hang onto their credibility. Without it, as we have indicated before, their ability to do their job is gone. A second purpose is to provide an overview of the spokesman and his or her relation with the law. Having said that, it is not my intent to discuss in explicit detail all matters relating to public relations and the law.

As has been written many times before, ours is a most litigious society. Statistics from the United States Department of Justice show that civil lawsuits far outnumber criminal cases (2013). For those who operate largely in the public spotlight—and this definitely includes organizational spokesmen and women—such a reality should raise eyebrows. If you mess up in front of hundreds, thousands, or even millions of people, one likely result is finding yourself involved in a lawsuit. This is one reason why it is essential that all public relations practitioners and professional communicators need to familiarize themselves with the law as it applies to them and what they do for a living. Unfortunately, as shown in past surveys, many practitioners have confessed to be lacking in such knowledge (Fitzpatrick, 1996).

The Values of the Public Relations Society of America

To begin, I start with the public relations profession itself and what steps it has taken to help ensure the proper conduct of its practitioners from an ethical standpoint. These apply to those serving in the spokesperson capacity as well. This is encapsulated in the code of ethics that was created by the Public Relations Society of America (PRSA), by far the largest professional organization in the profession. It has members throughout the world. Specifically, PRSA's code of ethics applies to its thousands of members and serves as a statement of professional values. It has undergone several updates and rewrites since it was introduced in 1948. The most recent version was produced in 2000. The general thrust of the code is that it urges PRSA members to not engage in any practice that corrupts the integrity of public communication or runs counter to that which is in accordance to the overall public welfare (Steel, 1966).

PRSA's code speaks to six primary values: advocacy, honesty, expertise, independence, loyalty, and fairness (PRSA, 2000). Briefly, advocacy speaks to working within the public interest by providing a voice in the marketplace to aid in informed public debate; honesty speaks to adhering to the highest standards of accuracy and truth; expertise calls for responsible use of knowledge and experience; independence calls on members to be accountable; loyalty says that members should be faithful to those they represent; and fairness says that practitioners should support the right of free expression. To enforce these values, PRSA calls on its members to report any fellow members whom they view as violating any of the guidelines set forth in the code of ethics. In terms of PRSA, the highest penalty that can be levied against a member is that his or her membership is revoked. If this were to happen, such a person could continue practicing public relations but not as a member of PRSA.

Obviously, if a practitioner violates PRSA's code of ethics to the extent that his or her behavior actually runs up against the laws of the United States, the consequences are much more extreme than simply being booted out of a professional organization. Suppose, for example, a communicator who works for a candidate for public office is given the assignment of writing a press release that says the opponent is a convicted child molester? As a loyal employee, you do it. The press release is picked up by the press. The opponent sues on the basis that this claim is false. Two questions: Can the communicator who was given the assignment be part of that suit and, even worse, be penalized by the courts for his or her actions? Or is the candidate who gave the communicator the assignment the only one who can be held accountable for this action? The answers are straightforward. The communicator can most definitely be named in a lawsuit as a co-conspirator and, in the same vein, be convicted. It is not a defense to claim, "I was just following orders." Any actions taken by a professional communicator, including the spokesman, are in concert with the client or those he or she represents. Consequently, this is where the risk of conspiracy comes into play (Simon, 1978). This scenario applies to spokesmen as well. If a press secretary, for instance, is directed to make a controversial claim about another person or ordered to give misleading information about a product, he or she, too, is vulnerable to being named as a co-conspirator in a lawsuit.

As identified by Newsom, Turk, and Kruckeberg (2013), there are three primary areas where public relations practitioners are particularly vulnerable: normal legal exposure as in matters of civil and criminal matters; work-oriented legal exposure regarding such areas as promotion, special events, and handling a crisis; and extraneous legal exposure that ranges from testifying as an expert witness to not registering as a lobbyist to not report-ing income and expenses for such activities. Of the three, the third most readily applies to the spokesperson as, more than the others, it involves providing public testimony on behalf of others and possibly being remunerated for it. Further, legal involvement for professional communicators has increased due to outsourcing. This tends to generate more contract work for public relations types, including those hired to serve as spokesmen. Organizations, of course, have always been responsible for the actions of their employees. The individual employees are also responsible for their own actions. As the profession of public relations has its functional roots in commercial speech, advertising, traditional speech, and the press, the legality of PR professionals' behavior remains linked to the laws that govern those areas (Huttenstine, 1993).

Commercial Speech and Political Speech

These two forms of speech relate to the spokesman or anyone else who speaks out on behalf of a product or person. *Commercial speech* pertains to matters of helping with marketplace transactions, while *political speech* refers to expression associated with the conduct of de-mocracy. Generally, the courts have taken a more lenient perspective on political speech than they have on commercial speech. This is because of the national commitment to the principle that the debate on public issues should be wide open, even if sharp attacks are part of the mix (Guth & Marsh, 2009). In reference to commercial speech, for many years the courts did not even see it as coming under the protection of the First Amendment. Recently, in *Central Hudson Gas & Electric Corporation v. Public Service Commission of New York*, the United States Supreme Court did determine that there are times when restrictions on commercial speech are necessary, as they serve certain social interests (1980). What dis-tinguishes commercial speech from political speech are usually the intended audience and the purpose of the message being put forth. Either way, it is often the spokesman who serves as the sender of that message. Thus, the message must be accurate or the messenger is in potentially murky waters, as in each case there are legal parameters that must be respected.

Defamation and Libel

Defamation and libel are two legal terms that pop up frequently in matters of communica-tion. Both speak to causing a person to suffer harm as a result of a malicious and/or false statement made against them (Harkin, 2008). *Defamation* pertains to the spoken word, while *libel* refers to written, broadcast, or other published works. Again, these are both scenarios that can and do involve organizational spokesmen. As Guth and Marsh (2009) so nicely explain, if a public relations practitioner is going to bad-mouth someone, either on his or her own or by assignment, he or she had better have the facts in order. Any time a person's public, personal, or professional reputation is challenged, the potential for legal challenge or dispute is always possible.

It should be noted that matters involving public officials are different than they are for others. Specifically, in the famous case of *The New York Times v. Sullivan* (1964), the Supreme Court ruled that public officials claiming to be libeled had to demonstrate or prove that the source of the statements against them knew or should have known they were not true. This higher burden of proof is known as *actual malice*, which the court defined as a knowing falsehood or reckless disregard for the truth. Since that ruling, the court has expanded the actual malice burden to libel cases involving public figures. Society, generally, includes celebrities and those well known to the general population as falling under the definition of public figure. As an aside, fairly or not, in cases of libel, public officials and public figures generally have not done well in the courts.

Ethical Behavior

A little earlier we looked at the code of ethics for public relations practitioners as crystallized by PRSA. This association, of course, is one of many that has put forth standards of behavior for its members. Such codes represent the both the highest and lowest standards of practice expected of the practitioner—all designed to present the profession he or she represents in a morale light (Levy, 1974). This readily applies to spokesmen who carry out their duties for themselves but on behalf of their organizations and clients. Their job is not just about them. It is also about others. The result is that they must be especially sensitive to behaving in a manner that leaves no doubt that they are firmly committed to honesty, fairness, and accuracy. Ideally, there must be no doubt among those who work with them, those who follow their actions, and those who use them as a resource that they maintain a high degree of professional integrity.

Having said that, one might ask, how this can be done if that same spokesperson is expected to speak out on behalf of a particular cause or issue, even to the point of being critical of positions at variance to what they endorse? Should not people with high integrity be open to what others say rather than critical or even indifferent? My answer is a resounding yes, though I quickly acknowledge that we do not seem to see or hear this much in today's world. For instance, watching many cable shows in which guests appear on behalf of candidates, clients, and issues, we are exposed to a great deal of passionate advocacy but little meaningful communication. The unfortunate result is that what begins as conversation between the guest and the host dissolves into little more than noise that, at best, validates those who already agree with the advocate rather than enlightens those wishing to learn more about the issue at hand as well as participate in future dialogues about it. The irony is that so many of the advocates who appear in the media end up turning off or turning away listeners and viewers who might actually be receptive to what they are saying. While these spokesmen and women possess conviction, so many seem to lack the wisdom needed to be effective communicators. Sadly, conviction without wisdom is little more than one-sided noise.

As is the case in all professions or walks of life, there are those who are better at their job than others. For instance, in the medical profession there are some doctors who are better than others. They either are better skilled, have a broader range of knowledge, are better communicators, or are more committed to adhering to the values that define their profession. It is no different in the communication profession. There are some public relations practitioners who function under the high calling of advancing communication. This, as we discussed earlier, is one of the primary values of PRSA. While all communicators use their skills to communicate specific messages, their challenge is to do so in a way that encourages exchange rather than stifles it. The trick here is to build bridges and strive to maintain them rather than simply out-argue others to the point that those who disagree or hold other perspectives do not wish to participate in a dialogue at all. If a so-called communicator achieves that, at best, they may have "won the day," but, at worst, compromised any opportunity to advance collaboration and mutual advancement. As people who function in the public arena, spokespeople have a social contract with society. This cloak places a set of expectations on them, which they are expected by the public to honor, even as they often speak on behalf of one entity over others. These expectations, not surprisingly, include being fair, honest, and straightforward, even while acting primarily in their own self-interest, as businesses largely do (Pratt, 2006). The spokesperson, of course, facilitates this yet, ideally, seeks to present the client as accepting social values as part of its mission (Davis, 1973).

This, then, brings us to explore ethics as they apply to organizational spokesmanship. The first step is to determine what ethics are. One succinct definition as put forth by Guth and Marsh (2009) is that *ethics* are values in action. Ethics represent a level of active adherence to what we believe. Ethics are not so much a to-do list for us to address each day, but more a core guide on how we conduct ourselves on a personal and, in this case, professional level. Even Aristotle viewed being ethical as a matter of sustained action that must be pursued rather than safeguarded. He believed that being ethical is searching for the highest good rather than just what is good (Heinaman, 1995). Happiness and living well, according to Aristotle, are two components of exhibiting ethical behavior. Obtaining them, however, is a constant and ongoing challenge that represent virtuous efforts on the part of those wishing to be viewed as ethical.

What is viewed today as relational ethics has evolved out of Aristotle's original thinking (Gilligan, 1982). It speaks to the matter of the connection between one's self and others and developing a proper appreciation of the way in which such universally recognized "goods" as friendship and pleasure are achieved and maintained. As Hill (1980) also voiced, ethical behavior rests within shared interest. Thus, for the individual spokesman and the entity he or she represents, actions and words or messages must not only be perceived to match but do so in reality, especially if they are to enjoy positive ties with others (Koten, 1986). With professional communicators, including spokesmen, being in the relationship business, each day they have the dual challenge of conducting themselves in an ethical manner but also helping ensure that their organization does so as well. This, perhaps, is one reason why people in public relations are sometimes referred to as being the "conscience" of organizations and management (Newsom, Turk, & Kruckeberg, 2013). In the case of the spokesman, if he or she is going to be the one that defends or speaks on behalf of those he or she represents, it behooves all concerned that management and their communicators behave ethically as well.

All this sounds pretty simple—right? Unfortunately, behaving ethically is not always as straightforward as it might appear. Those who serve as spokesmen are expected to be advocates for their clients or organizations. Thus, their bottom-line task is to persuade others to agree with and/or accept the actions and decisions of their entity. But can this be done in a way that continues to encourage dialogue? The answer is yes, though this is not to say it is always easy. When we are confronted by a person who disagrees with us, it is not uncommon for us to wants to out-argue that person until he or she either comes around to our way of thinking or at least concedes that our perspective is valid. Drawing from the philosophy of Aristotle, ideally, the greater good in such a scenario is not to win the argument. Rather, it is to respond to the questions and counterarguments in a way that encourages greater verbal interaction. As Aristotle suggested, debate and dialogue are not mutually exclusive. Dialogue leads to relationship, relationship leads to collaboration, and collaboration leads to shared progress.

The organizational spokesman is in a key position to make this happen. By viewing questions and verbal challenges as opportunities to enhance ties with others, the spokesman can both present talking points and build bridges. This starts with attitude and a core conviction on the spokesman's part that communication is most effective when it contributes to partnership. It happens when the spokesman refrains from name calling, disrespecting others, giving out false or misleading information, not validating other perspectives, and being inaccessible.

At the beginning of this text, I wrote of Jerald terHorst, press secretary to president Gerald Ford, who resigned as a result of Ford's decision to grant a full pardon to former president Richard Nixon. terHorst made the decision he did as he felt his ability to communicate—build bridges—on behalf of the president had been compromised. Though perhaps the most dramatic case of a press secretary making such a choice, it is not the only example of a highly visible press secretary finding himself with a similar ethical dilemma. In March 2010, the press secretary to then–governor of New York David Paterson was asked by her boss to take a certain action that she believed would compromise her credibility with the media and general public. Governor Paterson asked Marissa Sorenstein, his press secretary, to contradict earlier press reports about a staff member involved in a domestic violence case that were known to be true. Sorenstein saw her boss as ordering her to lie. She refused and resigned.

In November 2007, the superiors to Aaron Walker, the press secretary for the Federal Emergency Management Agency (FEMA), decided to have a press conference regarding California wildfires. Media were given very short notice for this event. In fact, it was so short that none showed up in person at the designated time and place. (This has happened to me. Scheduling a press conference and having no reporters show up is quite embarrassing. At the same time, having a press conference and having the room filled with members of the press is quite exhilarating.) Several reporters did "attend" Walker's press conference but only from a remote location. To make for a better appearance, Walker had FEMA staff members attend the gathering, pretending to be reporters. They were given questions to ask and proceeded to do so. The legitimate members of the press who participated via remote locations were only able to listen to what was being said. They were not able to ask questions of their own. It did not take long for word to get out that this had been a fake press conference, made only worse because it was papered with fake reporters asking self-serving questions. Walker quickly resigned. He expressed regret at his decision regarding the press conference, as he recognized it had done harm to FEMA's reputation and to his own professional credibility.

Without question, the incidents regarding Sorenstein, Walker, and terHorst were not so complex as to represent a Gordian knot (so complex that it could not be untied). In each case, in fact, the so-called knot did not need to be untied, as doing so was not necessary. From the perspective of each of these press secretaries, the ethical question at hand was quite solvable. Unfortunately for them, their solutions meant stepping down from their jobs. As public leaders, each felt they had a responsibility to do what they deemed to be the right thing. They made choices that not everyone in a similar situation would have made. After all, there remains no scientific way to study and define what is the most "correct" interpretation in any given situation (Gortner, 1991). But the decisions made by the three at least addressed their sense of ethical correctness. In addition, the ultimate choices by terHorst, Sorenstein, and Walker reflected values that typified the best values of the agencies from which each resigned. Thus, in stepping down, they were being loyal to the very entities they decided to leave.

Finally, the three displayed a strong sense of professionalism that helped them confront the dilemma of professional ethics that they felt they faced. In such matters, particularly those involving employees such as press secretaries who work in the public arena, four issues apply (Bayles, 1989): a goal of equal service to all, the relationship between clients or public and professionals, the impact on others of professional conduct on behalf of clients, and the professional's status as an employee. It was this kind of rounded thinking that drove the ultimate decision by Sorenstein, Walker, and terHorst. In today's climate, their interpretation should continue to prevail. Because of their proximity to the public, organizational spokesmen are public servants—even if they technically work for the private sector. Thus, the effectiveness is determined not by how they are perceived by their superiors or fellow workers but also by members of the public, including the media. These internal and external publics help determine that communicator's success. From an ethical standpoint, this is why it is to the spokesman's advantage to maintain and encourage open lines of dialogue with them and to be seen as a leader in that effort.

On a final note regarding ethics, there is a matter of trust. The question is not only whether the spokesman is credible, but whether this person is trustworthy. The two concepts overlap but are also distinct in that *credible* refers to one's level of expertise, while *trust* speaks to believability. Trust represents a foundation of society because communities cannot operate or interact without it (Fukuyama, 1995). In essence, it is a glue that defines virtually every social interaction in which all of us participate (Botan & Taylor, 2005). This includes receiving information from a press secretary.

Chapter Highlights

- The Public Relations Society of America (PRSA) is the largest professional association in the communication profession. In its code of ethics, among the values to which it subscribes are honesty and fairness.
- Organizational spokesmen are not above the law. They, too, can be held accountable for communiqués that libel or defame other parties.
- To maintain the confidence of their publics and be viewed as credible, organizational spokesmen need to adhere to the highest standards of honesty and transparency.
- A significant challenge for the spokesman is to advocate on behalf of the organization or client while encouraging dialogue with those who might challenge or question what it is the spokesman is saying.
- Being ethical is a daily challenge that must be pursued continuously.
- The spokesman must strike a balance between representing the interests of the client with demonstrating that the client is acting in the best interests of the general public.
- The spokesmanship needs to be both credible and trustworthy.

Discussion Questions

- Is it possible for a spokesman to be both an organizational advocate and a proponent of dialogue with others? How does one strike this balance?
- Do you agree with court rulings that communicators can and should be held accountable for any misinformation they are instructed to disseminate?
- Do you feel it was necessary for Aaron Walker to resign after staging a pseudo press conference? How was this different from a staged media event that organizations often organize?
- Do you agree with the court's interpretation that public figures should carry a burden of proof larger than nonfamous people when claiming they have been libeled?
- Can you see any circumstance that might cause you to resign your position, similarly to what Jerald terHorst and Marissa Shorenstein did?
- How important to an organization is maintaining a dialogue with its various publics?
- What are strategies a spokesman can follow that demonstrate that the client cares as much for the overall public welfare as it does with advancing its own agenda?
- Is it possible for a press secretary to be credible, yet not be trustworthy?

FOCUS ON

Jeff Rosenblum, Founding Partner of Questus

Widely regarded as one of the leading innovators in the field of digital marketing, Jeff Rosenblum has called a pioneer, a disruptor, and, in his own words, "a pain." Recently, he put the finishing touches on *The Naked Brand*, a documentary film about the future of advertising. It reveals the surprising story of the industry's ability to help save the planet one step at a time. To put it together, Rosenblum traveled the world to interview industry visionaries, scientists, authors, and CEOs.

As founding partner of Questus, Rosenblum focuses on developing processes that break down the boundaries that exist between research, strategy, and creation. He brought this multidisciplinary philosophy to help the Questus team produce industry-changing results for such leading brands as Capital One, General Mills, the National Football League, and Suzuki Motorcycles.

As an industry thought leader, Rosenblum contributes regularly to *Ad Age* and *iMedia Connection*. He has also been featured in *Newsweek* and on Bloomberg TV. In addition, he presents at industry conferences, including iMedia, IAB, Shop.org, Webcom, Adweek, and Game Changers, and has been a guest lecturer at New York University and the London Business School.

Presently, Rosenblum serves on the advisory board for the New York chapter of the Make a Wish Foundation. Over the past few years he has led initiatives to use digital marketing to help the foundation raise millions of dollars online.

Question: In so much of your work you help clients with messaging. Could you talk a bit about the process that goes into that?

Answer: There are many similarities between advertising and the role of the spokesman. In fact, we see discussions going on about which one is responsible for what duties. For instance, is Facebook advertising or public relations? One of the key areas of focus for the next generation of communicators is to break down the internal silos that exist in many organizations and corporations. I also feel there needs to be a new set of titles signifying a new kind of responsibility. Chief listening officer is one. Another would be chief silo buster. Those may sound funny, but in so much of the communication world today there needs to be greater collaboration and far less turf battles. This must happen for any entity to have a chance at a successful future.

Without question, the number-one issue facing organizations is learning to compete in the age of transparency. Our documentary *The Naked Brand* was driven by that. Companies are now naked. Years ago, the spokesman was viewed by how eloquent, charismatic, or attractive they were. Now the spokesman is the lens of the organization or their client. All the eloquence in the world cannot cover up a brand's behavior. Great brands are built by being great, not just by saying they are great.

From an advertising perspective, companies could pretty much behave any way they wanted. They would come up with a super catchy jingle, and that would be enough for people to fall in love with the image projected by a company. More and more that is no longer the case. Nike is a perfect example. In the late 1990s, their poor labor practices were revealed. Their workers in other countries were treated poorly. It raised the question: What does Nike really do? What kind of image and lifestyle was Nike projecting? When they were outed, Nike lost millions of dollars. Interestingly, what they lost turned out to be about what they were spending on marketing. They found they could not overcome the negative perceptions regarding their behavior. None of that happened because of technology.

There are upwards of 30 billion pieces of information on Facebook every month. To me, the most important ones are the ratings and reviews posted by consumers. Social reviews. If you look at restaurant reviews posted by regular folks, you find them to be amazingly accurate. Television ads are becoming increasingly ignored in terms of impact. We are finding recommendations by friends or even strangers to be much more trusted than ones found in advertisements.

This is true of spokesmen. It is not enough for them to be extremely articulate or appealing to watch. In what they do they need to be on the side of fostering transparency. This is true for government agencies, the private sector, and higher education. They, too, are in an age of transparency. Any government that embraces transparency is going to win. Granted, you will find a bunch of people who disagree or hate what you are doing. But, at the same time, if you are more open, you will also find those who instantly agree with that and, as a result, are happy to carry forth your vision. The key here is credibility. The key to any great brand is trust. In my own research, I have looked at companies that have embraced transparency, including Apple and Chipotle. Their financial performances are overwhelming. For any entity, it can no longer be a question of whether you should be transparent and open. This mind-set must be part of the company's overall vision.

Another example is Patagonia. This company is doing very well. Interestingly, (this change is fine) they included on their website in which they voluntarily disclosed some negative things that happen in the manufacturing of their supply chain. It pertained to the negative impact on the environment. Patagonia was open about this and then proceeded to report what they were doing about it. I found this out as a potential customer, as I had gone on their website to purchase a jacket. When I read this information, I decided not to make a purchase, but because of their openness, they turned me into an evangelist for their company. I am now a big supporter who carries their message to my friends and family because of their transparency. Sure, at that moment they lost a sale, but they also gained so much more.

The lesson here is that brands are built on behavior. People are responding to this much more than to what companies and organizations are saying about themselves. Apple is another example. They present themselves from the consumer's perspective. This has worked tremendously well for them, as it removed friction between audience and brand. They did and still do this by giving their customers a good real-world experience. Their success is based on greatness of product and absence of friction.

Question: Earlier you mentioned breaking down internal silos. Can you talk more about this?

Answer: Whether from the perspective of the spokesman or the advertising agency, the conversation between product and consumer has been turned upside down. Internally, it is no longer good enough for the spokesman to look to his client and say, "What do you want me to say?" Now, the spokesman examines what is good or bad about their client's behavior and provides guidance as how it either should be changed or promoted. They do this on the basis of several fundamental questions: who, why, and what?

The "who" refers to asking, "Who are we trying to appeal to?" Let's find the targeted audience we are trying to appeal to. This will help you create more loyal customers.

They "why" speaks to why will people not only shop for our product or utilize our services, but why will they evangelize for us? This comes down to a lot less of the product and more of what the brand we are projecting stands for. Why are we in business? What are we doing to improve the real-world experience of our customers?

Finally, "where" goes beyond purchasing full-page ads in magazines or standing in front of a podium and being glib. It taps into behavior and putting forth an effort to turn customers into evangelists on our behalf. Turning points of pain into points of pleasure.

Communication has been disrupted by technology. Companies and organizations that rely on brands are becoming antiquated. The key is found in behavior relating to how one goes about their business and how transparent that behavior is to others.

Source: J. Rosenblum (personal communication, December, 2012, 2013).

Chapter Five

The Road to Spokesmanship

One of the significant trends in the field of public relations over the past 20 years is that the path to pursuing a career in this growing field has become more clear. A great many more universities and colleges throughout the United States are offering designated programs in public relations and communication programs, enabling students to graduate with qualifications often deemed strong enough to attain jobs in the profession. In addition, many of these programs include in them opportunities for students to acquire paid internships designed to provide them with valuable real-world experience. The result is that not only has the number of practicing professionals increased but national projections indicate that these numbers will continue to do so. The academic programs train and educate the prospective professional communicators in areas ranging from crisis, risk, and sports communication to marketing, health, and strategic communication. Make no mistake: this is all good because so many of these specific areas speak directly to societal needs in public relations and communication. Thus, the more qualified students produced by institutions of higher learning, the more this benefits companies, business, associations, and organizations that rely so strongly on developing vibrant communication mechanisms for the sake of their successful survival and growth. In a nutshell, it is a win-win for all concerned.

But what about the specific area of organizational spokesmanship? What is available to those students wishing to pursue a career in this exact aspect of public relations? At present, there is little available to them. There are programs giving students a chance to pursue careers in health communication and others to move toward one in sports informa-tion, to cite two examples. But when it comes to organizational spokesmanship, a specific academic path has not yet been defined. The result—currently—is that communication students are not able to major or minor in spokesmanship or gain the academic credentials that speak directly to what makes one qualified to be a press secretary. At least not yet.

This observation should not be interpreted as a criticism of our universities and colleges or the communication scholars that help give them distinction. After all, the truth is that is there not is a clear, direct path toward becoming a press secretary or organizational spokesman once one is firmly entrenched in the field. Following conversations with men and women who currently serve as their organization's spokesperson, my own unscientific observations, and even my own career path, my present sense is that I am sure any public relations or communication department would be hard-pressed to design a program of study providing students with a direct path that takes them from graduation to spokes-manship. The focus of this chapter, then, is to explain why that is the case while identifying qualities a prospective spokesperson needs, so that if and when the stars align themselves in a certain way, this person can step into the role of spokesman or press secretary.

My Journey

I begin by sharing my own journey. But in telling my story, I should immediately note that I do not consider it typical or one that others should necessarily try to replicate. At the same time, I do not contend it to be unique or anything others could not do. To me, the only thing that does make it special is the fact that it is mine. (Note to readers: I recognize that my story may not be the most enthralling one to read, so I promise not to make it any longer than is necessary.)

As far back as high school I have enjoyed writing. While I dabbled in poetry, without question what I enjoyed most was the challenge of telling the stories of others far more. I enjoyed getting them to talk about things from their perspective in a way that captured not only what they had to say but a little bit of them as a person. My outlet was the high school newspaper. My school was Woodlawn High, located in Baltimore County, Maryland. Perhaps because I was a member of several of the school's sports teams, I primar-ily wrote for the sports page. Looking back, the fact I rode the bench in most every sport I played probably helped my budding career in journalism, as I was able to gain exclusive interviews with the stars of the various teams. It just occurred to me that, technically, one could say I gained good experience in multitasking: riding the bench and writing. Also, I do not recall writing anything back then that was particularly impressive, but nevertheless I still received a good number of bylines.

From high school I went to college: the University of Tennessee in Knoxville. My major was—what else?—journalism. My career ambition was to become a newspaper reporter. Within a few days of being dropped off by my parents I found my way to the univer-sity's student newspaper and volunteered to join its writing staff. Much to my surprise and delight, the paper accepted my offer. UT's paper was *The Daily Beacon*. Because of the institution's student enrollment, it was one of the biggest newspapers in Tennessee. (I never stopped trying to impress people with that piece of information.) I wrote for the paper my entire time at UT, until I graduated in 1972. During my 4 years there, campus police, student life, and the administration were among my beats or assigned areas of coverage. During my final semester at UT, I even served as the paper's managing editor. Approximately 1 month before graduating, I was fortunate enough to land a job as a general assignment reporter at the *Clarksville Leaf-Chronicle* in a small town just north of Nashville.

Reporting to duty at the *Leaf-Chronicle*, I felt more certain than ever that this was the beginning of a long career in journalism. I worked there a little over a year. In covering such areas as the city and county governments, traffic, and police, my exposure to interviewing others, collecting information, and trying to share it with others in a way that was concise and understandable continued to grow. Looking back, was I any good? While in all fairness, I certainly had some positive moments, overall I would give myself a rating of "fair." From the *Chronicle*, I took a new job at a newspaper in Hagerstown, Maryland: the *Hagerstown Morning Herald*. While there, I covered a number of municipalities, the police, and even local politics.

As was the case at the *Chronicle*, I do not recall doing much to distinguish myself. But does what stand out in my mind is that during my time at the *Morning Herald*, I remember becoming increasingly aware of public relations officers and media representatives. It seemed that with increasing frequency in my effort to cover stories, I found myself interacting with people whose job it was to work exclusively with reporters and speak on behalf of those with whom I wanted direct contact. While my fellow reporters would mock and sometimes make disparaging comments about "those PR flacks," I found myself being drawn to the challenge of their work. I also found them to be helpful in explaining stories I did not quite understand and even arranging interviews for me with key leaders in and around Hagerstown. Plus, I found their work schedules to be quite appealing. When I worked for a morning paper, my regular workweek was Tuesday through Sunday, 1:00 to 10:00 p.m. That is a schedule I never got used to. I remember being envious of the more "normal" work schedule of the media reps: Monday through Friday, 8:00 or 9:00 a.m. to 5:00 p.m. It was a combination of what I call "schedule-envy" and feelings of doubt as to whether journalism was, in fact, my life's calling that led me to begin looking for other career options. A possible career in public relations seemed like a strong possibility.

I remember being struck even then by how similar the work of a reporter and the work of a public relations representative were. The two seemed to have much in common. (Over the past nearly 40 years since my time at the *Morning Herald*, I would say that similarity has only increased. I will set aside the discussion of whether that is good or bad for another day.) First and foremost, the two have to be good communicators. This includes being able to write well, work well with others, work within deadlines, and be accurate in what they do. Furthermore, their jobs are carried out in a fishbowl. For better or worse, everyone knows whether they have done well, as what they do is for public consumption. As a result, the two work under a constant stream of pressure. In terms of writing, the two also gear their communiqués to both general and, at time, specific audiences. And it is not uncommon for the two to depend on the other for information, assistance in reaching others, and even a degree of collaboration.

I determined that whatever skills I had acquired through college and working for several newspapers could be easily transferred to what I would be asked to do as a public relations officer. I began applying for whatever positions in public information or relations I could identify. At the same time I began taking graduate classes in communication at nearby Shippensburg State College in Pennsylvania. I felt college credit would complement my more than 2 years of work as a reporter. Once again, fortune was on my side, as I was able to land my first job in public relations. It was at Anne Arundel Community College located just outside of Annapolis, Maryland. Though the actual position was called assistant director of community relations, my primary function was to generate publicity for the college by helping prepare brochures, churn out press releases, and work with area reporters. It was the working with reporters aspect of my job that gave me my first taste of being a spokesperson. The person who hired me did not come from any kind of media background, so he was not able to give me much guidance in that regard, nor did he have interest in giving interviews or serving as a direct resource for the press. So, it was a combination of my media background and the fact no one else was available or willing to be that person as to why I became that institution's primary press liaison.

As this was a community college, we did not generate much media attention, though the local newspapers were very generous about running our press releases. However, this did not prevent me from talking with reporters who covered education on a regular basis. Doing so reinforced my knowledge of their work being deadline-driven and enabled me to learn what their specific deadlines were. This told me the times of day when it would be easier to reach them and the times when I needed to leave them alone. In my capacity as a non-reporter, I gained an even deeper appreciation of the work reporters do in seeking out stories to cover as well as a better understanding of the elements they look for in a potential story. These ranged from human interest and timeliness to locale and unusualness. Much of this has been identified in a range of texts on public relations over the past several decades. Wilcox and Reber (2013), for example, added conflict and newness to my list.

Earlier in the text I mentioned how one should be careful about press conferences. Such an event should be scheduled on only rare occasions. I learned this the hard way. The community college was planning to offer several new programs of study. I thought it would be great to have a press conference so that our president could make the announcement, thus getting positive visibility for himself and the institution. A date was set. Announcements were distributed. Follow-up phone calls to reporters were made. And press releases were prepared. The time and day came, and the only people present were us. No reporters showed. I was upset, disappointed, and surprised. Fortunately, my superiors, including the president, were sympathetic and told me not to worry about it. Of course, I did. I talked with each of my press contacts and was given the unanimous feedback that none of them deemed the press conference worth attending. The lesson I learned is that just because something may seem like a big deal to us—or me—does not mean that others see it that way, too. This experience also told me that I needed to do a better job of determining what reporters consider to be newsworthy.

I worked at Anne Arundel Community College for 6 years. Between then and 1989, the year I was hired as head of public relations for George Mason University, I worked at two other institutions of higher learning: Towson University and Howard Community College, both also located in Maryland. The jobs at these institutions were challenging and, most important, contributed greatly to my professional learning curve. Only a lesser part of my job at each place was to serve as spokesman. That was left mainly to administrators ranked higher than me. Still, I continued to be proactive in establishing and maintaining good ties with reporters and editors. I have continued this practice right up until today. There is nothing special or magical about establishing strong working ties with members of the press, even in this age of emails and social media. It requires reaching out, making office calls, and practicing respectful coopera-tion. For both them and public relations practitioners like me, it makes our jobs much easier.

Prior to joining the administrative team at Mason, my time spent serving as a spokes-man was limited and situational. That changed at Mason. Even though I was not called "press secretary," it was assumed and expected that I would be the one who handled all initial interview requests, communicated our talking points to reporters, and provided comment to the public on the university's reaction to pertinent issues that had impact on us. Thus, I stepped into that role without specific training. It was learn-as-you-go for me. Learn I did but not without trepidation—at least initially. That was 24 years ago. I confess even to this day that I still am nervous every time I step in front of a microphone or a reporter with a notepad. Will I be articulate? Will I remember all the correct information? What happens if I am asked an unexpected question? My internal uncertainty may say more about me than the job; I am not sure. But those feelings of insecurity have helped keep me focused every time I have been approached for an interview or called on to speak on behalf of my institution. How well I have done I will leave to others to determine.

I wish to conclude my story by recapping three case studies in which I was called on as organizational spokesman to participate. Each presented interesting challenges that, col-lectively, showcase the tightrope on which press secretaries often find themselves walking. They all occurred at George Mason University.

Case Study 1: Student Suicide

It was a quiet day in January 2007. The fall semester had ended the month before, and spring semester classes were not slated to begin for several more weeks. As a result, with relatively few exceptions, most members of the faculty and student body were not even on campus. Only administrative members were around to carry on the university's business. The time was shortly after noon. A 27-year-old man walked into the Johnson Center, the largest building on campus: 320,000 square feet, 8 acres of floor space, 4 stories high. The facility is a combination library–student union, with a food court similar to what one would find in a shopping mall. Generally, those in the building were gathering to have lunch. Without bringing attention to himself, the man made his way to the top floor. No one saw him go over the side of the heavy metal railings, but some saw his rapid descent. And a few saw him hit the concrete floor at the lowest level of the building. What happened quickly turned a quiet day into one of much activity.

Word spread quickly throughout campus that something terrible had happened in the Johnson Center. Just as quickly, as a result of listening to their police scanners, media picked up on the shocking tragedy. I was in my office at the time. I received a call that somebody had died in the Johnson Center but was not given any details beyond that. I went over and found the spot where the student had landed swarming with police. The young man, amazingly still alive, had just been rushed to an area hospital. (He died en route.) I gained what information I could from the police. At the time, they did not know much more than that a young man had been fatally injured from the fall. It was at this point when the reporters—television and print—began arriving.

Generally, when it comes to student suicide cases or ones where the possibility that a student has taken his or her life, my experience has been that the media tends to shy away. These situations are private matters, are painful to those close to the victim, and obviously involve a very troubled person. In this case, however, the fact what happened occurred in a very public setting and that the question of suicide had not yet been determined brought the media out.

Issues at Hand

As the spokesman, I recognized that this incident involved more than simply acquiring what information was available and sharing it with reporters. While that was certainly part of my initial challenge, there were other issues that needed to be addressed or dealt with great sensitivity. These included the following:

- *One Voice:* The last thing we needed or wanted was to have several people talking with reporters about what happened. This meant determining who would do the talking: a representative of the police, the university's spokesperson, a higher-ranking administrator, or one of the workers from the Johnson Center. While our policy was that I as the spokesman would do the talking, we still took the step of making sure such a policy was not being changed for this situation.

  The problem with having multiple sources is that is that it creates a potential that these well-meaning people might contradict each other. Plus, it creates confusion among reporters as to who is officially speaking on behalf of the organization. Thus, establishing an official voice helps reporters do their job. This, of course, does not prevent them from talking with whoever they want to on any given matter. In the case of this suicide, the press certainly did just that; but they did so with the understanding that no matter the number of accounts they collected, there was only one official voice.

- *Accuracy and Facts:* Everything revolved around this. A complete and detailed account of what transpired had to be attained. It was essential that I work closely with the police to receive information as they collected it.

- *Family's Privacy:* The victim was an adult. Thus, information about him was a matter of public record. However, as a matter of decency, being sensitive to his family drove our decision not to release his name. The last thing we wanted was the victim's immediate family to read or hear of his demise in the press. Thus, on behalf of the university, as spokesman I did not disclose his name. It should be noted that his name was made public, but that detail was not disclosed by us.

- *University's Reputation:* How an organization or institution handles an unexpected situation can have a direct impact on its public reputation. This is why it is essential that any public pronouncements a spokesman makes be done with a regard to how they will be received, along with an understanding of what the public is looking to hear, see, and learn. This is done by being in sync with your entity's publics. Developing a sense of the public's mood and level of receptivity does not happen overnight. It requires a sustained effort to talk with—not at—representatives of the public and listen, process, and understand what they say. This invaluable information enables spokespeople to identify with their audiences (Smith, 2009). Doing this enabled me to represent the university in a manner that best addressed its position in this manner as well as respond to the concerns and questions the media had and the public might have regarding us. This knowledge helped serve as an outline for how I presented the facts to reporters. It also helped ensure that I did this in a way that did not undermine our reputation or image. Questions from reporters paralleled the police's investigation: as the police uncovered more details, the reporters had more questions.

- *Investigation:* I did not in any way try to insert myself into work the police had to do. That would have been a big mistake on multiple levels: (1) I lacked the qualifications, (2) I would have gotten in their way, and (3) I may have threatened my positive relationship with them. I mention these points because when the media is demanding more information, sometimes there might be a temptation to begin applying equal pressure on those professionals who are trying to get to the bottom of the incident. Rather than do that, I established a "touch-base" schedule with the chief investigator, who provided me with the most current information that I could then share with reporters. This enabled me to provide the press with timely information in an efficient and orderly manner.

    My experience has been that reporters generally respond favorably to such a protocol. The challenge is to establish such a schedule, communicate it to as many people who need to know, and then honor it. This helps maintain good ties with the press and reinforces the spokesman's credibility.

    In terms of the actual findings, later in the day the police tracked down the car the victim drove to campus. In it, they found a suicide note. Police also reported that there was no negligence on the part of the university or sign of foul play.

- *General Public:* The student's act was a public tragedy. As a result of media attention, the question of whether the university should share details of the incident with the public and its stakeholders was not a matter of debate. The decision was made, however, not to issue an official statement to external audiences but rather let media coverage serve that role. As the spokesman in this matter, I did not receive any inquiries or calls from members of the outside public.

- *Internal Public:* As is the case with any institution of higher learning of significant size, George Mason has had more than one experience with student suicides. (Mason's current student enrollment is approximately 34,000.) Generally, when this happens, no effort is made to communicate or share information with the institution's 6,000 faculty and staff. The reason for this is twofold: to protect the privacy of the victim's family and close connections, and because the act is not considered to be a threat to the campus community. In this case of the student's suicide in the Johnson Center, information on what happened was shared with Mason's employees. As the student's act was carried out in such a public way and received a good deal of attention in the press, to not share details of what happened was viewed as being counterproductive. People were talking about it anyway. An official statement was deemed necessary to quell any rumors and spreading of false information.

Case Study 2: Final Four

Arguably, the most exciting event in George Mason's history was the men's basketball team performance in the 2006 National Collegiate Athletic Association (NCAA) tournament. The team entered the annual tournament as a dark horse. No one, including many at Mason itself, expected the team to last long in the tournament. The team proved the conventional wisdom wrong. They fought and scratched their way all the way to the tournament's coveted Final Four by upsetting a string of nationally ranked teams, including the one that won the NCAA tournament the previous year. During their winning streak, the team literally captivated much of the sports world, generating millions of dollars in free advertising as a result of massive media coverage. At one point, Mason and the team even were featured in a cover story in *Sports Illustrated* magazine. To put the attention of the team's success in perspective, in its more than 40 years as an independent university, two of the institution's faculty members have been awarded Nobel Prizes: one in 1986 and the other in 2002. As exciting and attention-getting as those times were, neither came close to generating the public and press response the 2006 men's basketball team did.

Issues at Hand

Not surprisingly, the successful run of the team kept the university's entire media relations team hopping. Media attention was relentless. Their demand for information about the university and the players and requests for interviews with everyone from students and the players to the president and the head coach was nonstop. It was exciting and overwhelming. In my capacity as organizational spokesman, it also created a number of unique challenges. Following is a review of the primary challenges:

- *Accuracy and Timeliness:* The more the men's team continued to win, the more media requests we received. Also on the receiving end of increased demands were the offices of alumni services and the bookstore, where Mason gear such as sweat clothes, bumper stickers, and office supplies bearing the Mason name and logo were sold. To help ensure the university maintained a reputation of being customer-friendly and professional, every unit at the university receiving a heavy volume of knocks at their door worked overtime in striving to be as cooperative as possible.

While the volume of requests was demanding in and of itself, there was also the matter of ensuring that all information about Mason that we distributed was accurate. Missteps, though understandable given the circumstance, in this regard could have compromised ongoing efforts to recruit students and maintain a positive visibility.

- *One Voice and Coordination:* The textbook game plan any time there is heavy media scrutiny is for one person to be designated as the primary spokesman on behalf of the organization or entity. In the case of the 2006 NCAA tournament, this conventional thinking went out the window. The media's demand to speak with such institutional leaders as the university president, the head coach of the men's basketball team, and other key administrators, including the head of admissions, made the notion of letting the traditional spokesman handle all inquiries irrelevant. Also, the volume of demands was too much for one person to handle. Plus, the nature of demands—one-on-one interviews—made traditional ways of handling multiple reporters such as press conferences, press briefings, or conference calls equally irrelevant. The result was a decision to go with multiple spokesmen, a strategy that created several challenges: coordinating the speakers, ensuring they worked from similar talking points, and deciding which spokesman would speak to which outlet.

  The coordination element was tricky because the team was playing its games at various locations throughout the country. This meant some of the people designated to be spokesmen were at those sites, while others remained on campus. The decision was made to let those traveling with the team, including the university's president and, obviously, the head coach, be the primary speakers for members of the press covering the games at their respective locations. These outlets included the major networks, wire services, major newspapers and magazines, and press local to those areas. The bulk of the media relations team, including myself, remained on campus and handled calls and requests from our local media.

  Examples of requests from the media ranged from exclusive interviews with the president and head coach to photo ops with students holding impromptu rallies at the statute of George Mason the Man located at the Fairfax campus. The timing of these and other requests would literally be at all hours of the day and night. We tried to be as accommodating and cooperative as possible with all of them.

- *University's Reputation:* This is always a concern, no matter what is going on. Over the years Mason has established a very positive reputation throughout its region and even the nation. As spokesman, safeguarding that and even seeking ways to enhance it is always part of my agenda. Even though the team's success in the NCAA tournament was a positive and happy turn of events, it also was deemed a potential threat. To begin, it had all the classic symptoms of a crisis: it was a surprise, it was a threat, and it required a short response time (Hermann, 1963). The tournament generated intense interest from the public, caused Mason to fall under great media scrutiny, led to Mason experiencing interference in its normal operations, and created threats to the institution's public image and economic stability). As Mason had no contingency plan for a circumstance such as the Final Four, actions and decisions taken by the administration were largely made from moment to moment.

- *Potential Threat:* When the unexpected occurs and no contingency plans exist, how does a spokesman know what to do or how to behave? Such a question is not as difficult as it might seem, particularly if well-defined guidelines are already in place. They certainly were for me and should be for any spokesman or press secretary. As we have already touched on, these guidelines include being accurate, accessible, timely, respectful of the media, mindful of the organization's or client's values and mission, and knowledgeable regarding the specific situation or incident. Taken together, they served as my North Star.
- *Welfare of Players:* If Mason's run to the Final Four in 2006 could be likened to a hurricane, the players on the men's basketball team were very much at its center. None of these young men had ever before experienced something of this nature. I can only imagine the pressure they must have felt. As part of the communication team that helped control access to them, our goal was to help ensure that they were protected from any unwanted advances from well-meaning, though aggressive reporters. We viewed each of the players as a Mason ambassador. Our challenge was to help provide them with the support they needed to relax—as much as possible—and play well.

Case Study 3: Sexual Misconduct

Even now, more than 8 years after this case came to light, I think back on it with sadness. In fall 2004, a fellow administrator at George Mason was arrested for extortion, possession of child pornography, and manufacturing child pornography. The arrest, which occurred on a weekend, caused quite a stir among his coworkers and generated a good deal of media attention. The facts of the case involved a respected university administrator who was arrested for taping sexual encounters with high school–age male students without their permission or knowledge and then attempting to use those tapes to blackmail his unsuspecting partners. His arrest came about when one of his partners told his parents, who then contacted area police. Their investigation revealed the existence of several tapes produced for purposes of blackmail. One of these encounters, it turned out, took place on a weekend afternoon in this administrator's office located in the university's administration building.

Media and public attention was immediate and high. Generally, they wanted to know the university's reaction, what role, if any, we would be playing in the police investigation, and even how we could hire someone of such questionable character in the first place. In dealing with the media and the general public, as in the other case studies, several challenges faced us.

Issues at Hand

- *Accuracy and Transparency:* Things happen. Mistakes occur. Sometimes they are unexpected and sometimes not. Generally, people understand that wrong turns occur. But what they have trouble reconciling is when entities or organization handle miscues with stonewalling, refusing to take responsibility, covering up the truth, suddenly becoming unavailable for questions from the public, or showing a lack of empathy to concerns expressed by the public. As spokesman, my challenge was to convey the opposite of those negative responses. The unexpected arrest of this administrator suddenly put into question the integrity of the university. I approached each inquiry from reporters with the goal of making sure Mason's reputation remained strong. Specifically, I assured reporters and members of the public that Mason was just as shocked at this man's arrest as anyone, that we were cooperating fully with police, that we were doing all we could to keep our students safe from any sexual predators, and that we were initiating a thorough review of our hiring practices to try and identify ways in which we hired only people of the highest character. I emphasized these points in each of my interviews with the press.

- *Internal Relations:* The nature of this case was very public. Much like the student suicide of the first case study, it generated a great deal of talk among all university employees. One of our communication goals was to keep to a minimum the spreading of false information or inaccurate rumors. Thus, we openly shared all information of the arrest and investigation with our staff, faculty, and students. We adopted the posture that we had nothing to hide.

- *Media Relations:* For the spokesman, this is always an issue. One never takes this professional relationship for granted, nor should they. These ties are only as strong as the last interview or press briefing. The stronger the relationship between press secretary and reporter, the more likely the reporter and the outlet he or she represents are to cover the spokesman's organization or client with a straightforward, open perspective.

- *One Voice:* The arrest of an administrator on such unsavory charges was something few, if anyone, wanted to talk about publicly. In this case, then, determining who would be available to speak to reporters was not an issue. Often, handling hot potatoes such as this case is what press secretaries do. Still, in this case reporters did talk with other staff members and students for their reaction to the arrest. Even with these interviews, the press knew who was the university's official voice.

Lessons Learned

Despite the obvious differences in the three case studies, they contained a number of similar challenges that in many ways characterize all situations that arise for the spokesperson and his or her organization. Being accessible to the press, establishing who is the official voice, protecting the organization's reputation, and being able to communicate with authority, knowledge, and empathy are among the commonalities. These components point to the lessons learned from those situations. They are ever-present as they apply to the day-to-day challenges of the spokesperson.

Building on the case studies and looking at the responsibilities of the press secretary, following is a "top-10" list of overriding lessons for the professional communicator who serves as the voice and face of the organization or client:

1. Every time while on the job, you are "on." The spokesperson does not have the luxury of kicking back and joking his or her way through interviews or giving half-hearted responses. The potential consequences—all negative—are too great.

2. Be professional and collegial with everyone with whom you work. It may seem like a lot of pressure to have to get on well with everyone, but such is the lot of the spokesman. On any given day, something may happen that brings you together with any office, department, or person within the organization. You may need to counsel others or elicit information or advice from them. Either way, you need their goodwill and ongoing cooperation, just as they need yours. Furthermore, these kind of positive ties enable you to better serve as a link between management and the workers.

3. There is an old adage that one must speak only when they have something to say. For spokespeople, they must speak publicly only when they know what they are talking about. If press secretaries, for example, are asked a question they do not know the answer to, they should say they do not know. If they are asked to speculate on something, they should avoid speculating or talking in hypotheticals. As people have a tendency to treat everything the person in front of the microphone says as fact, the spokesman needs to be sensitive to that and behave accordingly. Sticking to this helps establish your credibility and reputation as a teller of truth.

4. It may seem like it at times, but the press is not the enemy. Are they on your side? No. But they are not necessarily against you or your organization either. They, too, are communicators. Their job is to collect information and gain a solid understanding of it so that they can properly pass it on to others. Sometimes this involves asking what you might feel are questions you deem to be silly, annoying, or even confrontational. You, too, are an information gatherer. In order to prepare yourself to be interviewed by others, it is likely you, too, had to ask questions of your coworkers or superiors that they felt were silly, annoying, or even confrontational. Be as patient and open with the reporters as you want and need others to be with you.

5. For better or worse, we live in a world of appearance. People do make judgments on how one looks and behaves. Sometimes appearance and behavior can be so overwhelming that they take the focus off what is said. Do not let that happen. As a spokesman, your words are your ultimate currency. Inappropriate appearance or behavior cheapens your worth.

6. Information makes the world go around. Everyone needs and wants it, especially in times of stress or when facing the unknown. Often, as the spokesman, you are the one with that ever-so-desired commodity. The more you respect it and the more you present it in a way that is accurate, the greater service you are providing those who are looking to you for help so that they may cope with a given situation more easily and with greater understanding. These are no small things. Do not abuse your position as the person with the one thing everyone wants.

7. Having dual loyalties may seem like a tricky challenge. After all, how can any of us have equal loyalty to more than one ideal, person, or responsibility? Granted, this may not always be easy, but the fact is that we do this sort of thing every day. Let me explain by first identifying what the spokesman's dual loyalties are: your client or organization and the truth. Make no mistake, your job is to properly represent your entity in a positive light. Your job is also to communicate in a way that does not mislead or deceive. That is a major value for all professional communicators of high regard. Given these two

loyalties, what happens if certain circumstances arise that seem to put the two in direct conflict? Does the spokesman pick one over the other? The answer is an emphatic no! Be honest and upfront with your colleagues. If you anticipate being asked questions of a sensitive nature, the answers to which might do harm to those you represent, strategize on responses you can give that are neither harmful nor deceitful. Growing up, I was not the greatest student in the world. In fact, at times, my grades were borderline poor. At a family function, I remember my uncle asking my father how I was doing in school. My father smiled and said I was working to do better every day. The point here is that, in this moment, my father was loyal to both me and the truth. He was also very upfront with me about my low grades when only the two of us were talking.

8. People make mistakes. It is one of those things we as humans do on a pretty regular basis, even when we try hard not to. We communicate the best we can, but nevertheless we sometimes phrase things in a way that does not convey the intended meaning of our words. And then there are times when those to whom we are speaking misinterpret what we say. More often than not, these are honest mistakes. Granted, they can be aggravating, come at a bad time, or create unnecessary or unfair problems for others. As much as we can deal with these situations with grace and understanding, the better it is for everyone. If you as the spokesperson misstate something, correct the record as quickly as you can. If a reporter misquotes you, let that person know but in doing so give him or her the benefit of the doubt that the mistake was not meant with malice—unless you know otherwise. If that is the case, go to his or her editor.

9. Know your place. At times, as the person who is quoted in the newspaper or on the web or appears on television, every so often you may get to feel as if you are pretty special. We all do at times. And, of course, as my mother would say, all of us are special in our own way. (I am not about to argue with my mother.) But for the spokesman, the hard truth is that you are only as "special" as your organization allows you to be. Your job is to represent your organization or client. You are its front person. The truly special one in this relationship is the organization. Make no mistake. Your job is to serve it as well as you can. If this means that at times you feel as if you are walking on eggshells, it is because you are. Being a spokesman is not without stress. It is a job with pressure.

10. There is an old joke involving a person who is touring New York City. He goes up to someone on the street and asks, "How do you get to Carnegie Hall?" The person immediately responds, "Practice." Whatever talent you possess to be a spokesperson, never take it for granted. Keep practicing. Framing a specific message is an important aspect of the job, for example. Conduct mock interviews. Work on exactly how you might want to articulate or phrase certain statements or information. Again, going back to my mother, as good as you may be, you can always do better. This fact of life is no small thing.

The Proper Skill Set

No matter a person's chosen or hoped for walk of life, each one requires a particular skill and mind-set. The position of organizational spokesperson or press secretary is no exception.

Following is a list of demonstrated skills and perspectives that perspective press secretaries might consider and those looking to hire a competent spokesperson might look for:

- *Articulacy:* This speaks to being well spoken as opposed to glib or flip. Are you able to explain various issues in ways that are understandable? Are you able to respond to questions or comment in ways that focus on building bridges and greater unity of purpose?
- *Good Listening Skills:* This may seem like an odd skill for a spokesperson to have, but the fact is that it is a key ingredient to being successful and effective. Speaking to any segment of the population, including the media, is not just about the speaker. Without question, the speaker needs to know what he or she is going to say, but also needs to have a good sense of what is on the mind of the audience. What questions do they have? Concerns? Hopes? The speaker also needs to have a good sense of what is on the mind of those he or she represents. By this, I do not just mean the organization's chief executive or other top administrators. What about the secretaries, mid-level managers, or maintenance team? Their perspectives are important, too. In determining how best to frame messages or talking points, for instance, the more input the spokesman can generate, the better representative he or she will be. This wide input comes from listening to what others say. Just as the best writers are avid readers, the best speakers are strong listeners.
- *Confidence:* Stepping in front of a microphone or room full of reporters who are writing down everything you say is a lot of growing old—it is not for sissies. There is nothing with being nervous, of course. This just shows a desire to do well. The best way to gain confidence is to develop a strong understanding of your topic. Solid preparation contributes to equally solid performance.
- *Working Knowledge of Media:* Dealing with the media is often a daily part of the spokesperson's job. Getting to know the individual reporters, their interests, their deadlines, and their style of work contributes to having a positive working relationship with them. This often spills over into generating favorable coverage for your client.
- *Demonstrated Organizational Skills and Good Sense of Direction:* One of the most successful and variety shows in television history was the *Ed Sullivan Show*. Each week he would feature a wide variety of acts—some famous and some not. Every so often jugglers would appear who, as part of their act, would spin a number of plates on long, thin sticks at the same time. In all my years watching the *Ed Sullivan Show*, only rarely did I see any of those plates break. For the organizational spokesperson, his or her job can be a lot like spinning a number of plates at the same time. Being able to do that and do it well requires strong organizational skills, an ability to concentrate during intense times, and knowing how you wish things to proceed.
- *Demonstrated Flexibility:* Life being what it is, things do not always go according to plan or how we envision them. When this happens—and in the field of communication you can count on that being the case—flexibility and being able to think quickly on your feet are important skills to have. Again, preparation is the key to handling unexpected questions, for instance, or comments or actions from

those you represent. Not only being thoroughly up-to-date on the most current information but also knowing how that intersects with your organization's or client's overall mission and values helps give you the ability to be flexible.

This list is not meant in any way to be definitive. Depending on the specific organization, company, or client, specific qualities will need to be added or amended. It represents a suggested start.

Chapter Highlights

- At present, there is no clear path to becoming an organizational spokesman.
- There are numerous similarities between the work of a journalist and that of a public relations practitioner.
- Each situation facing the spokesman involves fundamental benchmarks that serve as a guide to help him or her communicate effectively.

Discussion Questions

- Should colleges and universities begin offering classes that help prepare communication students for careers as press secretaries? What kind of classes do you think they should offer?
- Can you think of other skills an organizational spokesman should have that you would add to the list that was started in this chapter?
- Can you identify examples in the news—past and present—that you believe were handled well and not very well by organizational spokesmen?

Focus On

Kathleen M. deLaski, President of the deLaski Family Foundation and Former Chief Spokesman for the Pentagon

Kathleen deLaski is president of the deLaski Family Foundation, a leading Washington, D.C., grant maker in education and the arts. She has spent 10 years in various roles working on education reform, most recently on the senior founding team for StudentsFirst, a national advocacy movement designed to create better school options, particularly for low-income families. She has also served as senior program officer for education at the Walton Family Foundation, where she managed a $130 million portfolio of nonprofit investments to grow advocacy capacity for education reform and quality public charter school seats across the United States. Previously, she was founding president of the Sallie Mae Fund, the nonprofit arm of student lending leader Sallie Mae, where she built a national education platform for low-income families to learn about financial aid and a $15 million to $20 million annual scholarship fund to support college access.

deLaski was named by president Bill Clinton as chief spokesman for the Pentagon, where she oversaw the military's worldwide public information team. She also spent 13 years as a television journalist, including 5 as an ABC News Washington correspondent, mostly covering politics and foreign policy.

deLaski earned her undergraduate degree in political science and English at Duke University and her master's degree in public administration at Harvard University's John F. Kennedy School of Government.

Question: You were a journalist before you got into public relations and began serving in the role of spokesman. How did that transition happen?

Answer: I had been a reporter for 13 years, mainly in television. I had worked my way from local to a national base. Working for ABC World News, at first I was more behind the scenes. My focus had been on such things as defense policy and international relations. Earlier, while taking classes at the Kennedy School of Government, I met a number of people who later ended up working in the Clinton administration. So, when I began working as a reporter, I ended up interacting with a lot of them.

Following President Clinton's election, his people began looking for someone who could serve as the public voice for the Pentagon. They were looking for someone at that point who knew the national press corps, had their respect, and had a good grasp of the defense issues. At the time I happened to be in Southern California. I received this call asking if I would be interested in leaving journalism and moving over into public affairs. They wanted to know if I would be interested in moving over to the other side.

Question: Was that a tough decision?

Answer: Actually, no. Their offer nicely coincided with negative feelings I was having about the press in general. I found myself growing more fed up with how much of the media was becoming particularly politicized. This was particularly true of television journalism. Covering the early Clinton administration, I could see the kind of "gotcha" mentality seeping in the coverage and work of reporters. The mentality of what passed for stories was becoming so very political. As part of it, there was also this notion that for a journalist to make a name for him- or herself, they had to wear their political leanings on their sleeve. This was not the way I came up or was trained. Before that phone call, I was becoming more and more discouraged about it all. I felt too many reporters were turning away from doing their jobs in an objective manner.

Question: This sounds as if this was the beginning of what we now call "niche journalism"?

Answer: I would say so, yes. It seemed to be the way of the journalistic pack. I wanted out of TV broadcast news. For me, the offer seemed a nice pathway out toward a more substantive environment. I felt more comfortable with working for the government—the Pentagon—as I believed it would give me a great opportunity to step out of what I felt was an increasing superficial world into one that was more substantive.

Question: Did you want to become a spokesman as you considered leaving journalism?

Answer: Yeah. I was thinking about that. I say that because, in part, I was a journalist. I was thinking about how I could parlay that into something that was meaningful and challenging. Becoming part of public affairs meant becoming a manager, a strategist, helping determine ways to communicate policy. As a spokesman, you are even a politician. The skill set and strengths I had acquired very much applied to this new offer. Journalism, you might say, helped prepare me for this new opportunity. It was important for me to know how to work the media. That was and is a nonnegotiable skill set for any spokesman in a government agency.

Question: How would you define "work the media"?

Answer: I say being able to work in their shoes; understand what they want. And, therefore, be able to balance what we want with what they want. At this point, I had relationships with many reporters. I had the mind-set of thinking like a journalist—a practical approach to media and public relations. I knew the media could be one's worst enemy or one's best friend. It is a matter of understanding them and being able to define your brand with them.

Question: So, you are representing a specific client and not representing a general audience as you would as a journalist?

Answer: Right. You are working for a particular organization. Before I joined the Pentagon, their relations with the press had been pretty combative. There was a lack of trust from the media. The press had a feeling the press office was trying to keep information from them. Rightly or not, that was the perception. It was a charged and difficult relationship. I worked hard at helping turn this around. Not to be so antagonistic. We would ask reporters to tell us what they needed and then do what we could to get it for them.

Question: Would you talk about the spokesman job itself?

Answer: One big aspect of it was to serve as chief communication strategist for the Secretary of Defense and state department. In doing that, you are also serving as spokesman for the broader military throughout the world. This meant working closely with the Joint Chiefs of Staff. Doing this required a lot of worldwide coordination. Also, in essence, you are running a publishing house—army information services, the FOIA [Freedom of Information Act] department, a public website, and all the digital assets at the time. It was very much a multipronged job. As you might guess, this involved a lot of traveling. We had a core number of reporters that traveled with us. We worked most closely with them.

Question: Would you say your job was more reactive or proactive?

Answer: It had always been more reactive before I came. Afterward, we tried to become more proactive in getting information out to the public and press. What I found it necessary to do was create a model in which I had a person manage a react-type news bureau. Everything that came at us this person was responsible for addressing. Then, I had someone in charge of proactive efforts. What did we want to get out there? What messages did we want to get out? My boss came in with a thoughtful agenda on what America's defense should look like after the Cold War. That was an example of a message we wanted to impart. There were, of course, other issues we wanted to talk about as well.

Question: I assume, then, one of your biggest challenges was balancing the reactive efforts of your office with the proactive side.

Answer: That's right. Reactive usually won. So much was going on in the world that people and the press wanted to know about. The Black Hawk down incident was one. Bosnia, Haiti, gays in the military were other issues of great importance.

At least 50% of the spokesman's job revolved around the briefings—giving them and preparing for them. We did so many briefings that were broadcast throughout the world. Normally, we would spend the entire morning preparing for them. This included anticipating questions, devising answers to them, and identifying specific points we might want to inject into our responses. We would ask each other questions, test each other. I would practice how I would respond. It was not like someone was telling me what to do or say. Rather, we all strategized together. I had to be careful not to get out ahead of the secretary with things I might share with the press, so I would check with him to make sure the information I might disclose was acceptable. I prided myself on not getting caught off guard too often. During briefings with the press, one thing you need to do from time to time is actually review your briefing book in front of them. They understood you may not know the answer to everything off the top of your head.

Question: What was your biggest worry?

Answer: Any spokesman's biggest worry is being put in a position where you come across as lying because you did not know about something that was going on and, as a result, end up giving out false information. That's why you try to couch your comments with "as far as I know" or something similar. Obviously, with the Pentagon, we dealt with a lot of touchy issues. It was vital that we maintain a reputation for being honest.

Question: What kind of skill set should a person wishing to become a spokesman have?

Answer: I would argue the best set of skills to have are those of a journalist, possibly even coming from that world. On the other hand, if you did an analysis of people working in the role today, you would probably find that is not the case. In today's world, public relations as a field of study is so much more popular. Journalism as a field of study seems to be declining. Plus, there are few jobs in journalism. It would be important to understand what journalists need: their deadlines, the type of stories they want, how to pitch a story to the press. You need to be a good storyteller, have an ability to sell, be a salesperson, a good writer, and be able to develop and communicate messages, manage ideas, and be able to design commentary to suit what you are trying to project and do so in a way that people understand. I think of it as having hard skills and soft skills. The hard skills would include journalism, organizational abilities, and being a good leader. The soft skills would include being a good listener, being compassionate, and being able to develop working relationships.

Question: As a spokesperson, who do you need to listen to and focus on?

Answer: For one, you have to listen to the journalists and be able to pick up on their vibe. You may not always be able to direct conversation with reporters, but you need to be able to identify what they want and need. You also need to be able to talk to the people within your internal chain of command to get ideas from them. If you have talked with a scientist about work they are doing, you then have the challenge of interpreting what they have done. This is not always easy, as you need to try and talk about it in a way that is interesting.

Question: Of course, not only are there reporters you are trying to connect with; there is their audience as well. What about them?

Answer: The consumer is definitely a factor. It is important to be able to talk with the average person. You may not know what the consumer specifically wants, but you need to hone in on that unseen person. This is a matter of getting to know your audience that is beyond the immediate press.

Question: This job sounds so stressful, especially since you are not master of what you communicate.

Answer: Yes. A lot of people look to you when things are not reported correctly. You could say you are responsible but not necessarily in charge. In part, it is a matter of working closely with the various elements within your organization in order to help ensure accurate information is communicated.

Question: Looking back, did you like the job of spokesman?

Answer: Oh, yes. It was one of my all-time favorite jogs. I found it simulating, challenging and important.

Question: When you watch spokesman today, what do you notice?

Answer: You don't always know what they have been authorized to say. But you can tell how much trust their boss has in them based on how comfortable they are with what they are allowed to say. I had to learn that you should not stutter or pause or speak in a dull voice. In the spokesman's world what you say is so much more important than how you say it. Now when I look at someone who speaks hauntingly, it suggests they did not have time to be briefed or are on thin ice when it comes to having a full grasp of the information they are trying to share.

Source: K. deLaski (personal communication, January, 2013).

Chapter Six

The Future

All of us need to be heard. Within us we carry a need to count, be understood, and even be accepted. These needs are part of Maslow's hierarchy of needs and serve as primary motivators for what drive us during the course of our days and lives (Maslow, 1954). Being heard is a principal way of gaining that acceptance or love. There are times, of course, when the voice we wish others to hear and accept may not actually be our own. Sometimes, that voice may need to be another's. It may present our sentiments and represent our positions, but it does not literally belong to us. Sometimes we are not in a position to speak for ourselves. As strongly as we may feel about something, there are circumstances where having others be our advocate or voice may be best.

Such a dynamic has been a reality since the beginning days of man. Advocates, defenders, emissaries, or representatives of others have been part of civilization in the form of lawyers, ambassadors, and even elected officials—to name a few—long before any of us came to be. Thus, the spokesman is a well-established fixture in our landscape and will continue to be. Ironically, in the one field in which one might expect the spokesman to have dwelled the longest—communication—this has not been the case. Despite the history of this area, the organizational or media spokesman (or press secretary) is relatively new. Furthermore, as part of its youth, it remains a role with little training or clear avenue by which to travel to attain. Those currently in the profession, including scholars and professional communication practitioners, have yet to pave a path. At present, such a vacuum helps define the spokesman role.

Two roads diverged in a wood, and I—
I took the one less traveled by,
And that has made all the difference.

The above passage represents the last few lines of Robert Frost's famous poem, "The Road Not Taken" (1919). When looking into the future as it applies to the role of organizational spokesman, what I see is a path not yet taken by those in the communication profession, nor those in organizations or related entities in executive positions who have the authority to hire press secretaries and establish their level of responsibilities. However, it is a path that is currently being considered with overtures to begin such a journey into the unknown already underway.

This is not to say, of course, that nothing has been done about the creation and filling of such a role. As we established at the outset of this text, that step has long been taken. What I am referring to is a path for those wishing to explore or pursue careers as spokesmen. That has not yet been attempted, even though the existence of such professionals is very much a reality. It is this very fact that makes the need for such a preparatory process. Of the many organizations utilizing the services of such a communication professional, my research revealed none that tapped into a well-defined pool to select the person to represent the organization before the public and media. The story of my own evolution into such a role that I shared in the last chapter is typical. I had no formal training. I took no established communication classes. When hired by the various places for which I worked throughout my professional career, the responsibility of being a spokesman was not even included in my initial duties or job description. In each case, I took on the role because no one else wanted it, there was no one else to do it, or an assumption was made that I had the skills because of my experience working with the media and in public relations.

Looking into the future, this important role and the organizations to which it belongs would be better served if the people filling it had better, more pointed training. It is this training that represents the path or road not yet taken by those with a vested or personal interest in the role of spokesman and the good it can bring. The ultimate goal would be producing highly trained and skilled spokesmen or press secretaries who are well coached in being able to serve as advocates yet in a manner that, ideally, fosters cooperation and harmony. Placing a person in the spokesman position simply because he or she may have a talent for "tit-for-tat" one-upmanship banter with other entities or with opposing spokesmen on an issue is short-term thinking at best. Debate and respectful disagreement are not bad things. But unless they lead to eventual compromise or meaningful consensus building, such exchanges are little more than negative noise sprinkled with sound bites. Ideally, spokesmen should be trained to participate in debate but with an open hand.

The fact that the role of the spokesman is being accepted by an increasing number of organizations in both the private and public sectors is a very positive step in the right direction. The challenge now is to create a mechanism by which prospective professional spokesman are educated and trained in such a way that they enhance public dialogue and interaction rather than stifle it. As our society grows and the challenges that all of us face become seemingly more complex, the last thing we need are glib, articulate men and women who carry out their duties wearing blinders. Yes, their job may be to serve as an advocate for an organization, individual client, candidate, cause, and so on, but that can and should be done to the betterment of others rather at their expense. In my view, inclusion trumps one-upmanship.

I concede that such a sentiment sounds great and is in many ways the kind of vanilla platitude that generates little disagreement. I also recognize that the practicality of it is difficult. Companies exist to make money. They hire people to help make that happen year after year. One of those professionals is a man or woman whose job it is to represent the company before the media and general public and who is able to answer questions, address issues, and even take on critics in a way that enhances the company's overall goal of making money and outperforming its competitors. This, after all, is part of the free-enterprise system. At the same time, as the primary functions of public relations officers are to persuade and create partnerships (Grunig & Hunt, 1984), what steps can universities and colleges—the two primary producers of future professional communicators—take to ensure that their graduates interested in working as press secretaries are able to perform these tasks in ways that include rather than exclude? Furthermore, much of the public relations leadership as well as the conventional wisdom of those in the profession dictates that such goals should be pursued in the context of social responsibility. Even if an organizational spokesman, for instance, cannot address all communication ills, he or she can at least not contribute to them. This truism is relevant in that public relations as a profession and as an act in today's world is nothing if not a driving component in the social fabric of society (Kelly, 1991).

People filling this role are often the front door to an entity. They play a vital role in helping shape public perception of the entity, ranging from a business or organization to a government agency or public personality. At this point, it does not matter whether it has been by happenstance or grand design—the spokesperson has emerged as a vital and perhaps even permanent dot on what I call the human landscape.

Recommendations

To address the above question, I am providing two sets of recommendations, one for individuals and one for institutions of higher learning. While the recommendations speak to these two categories, they also are designed to reinforce what I see as the permanent place of the spokesman in society. Also, the tone of the recommendations are different. Ones for individuals are more along self-improvement lines, while those for higher education speak to institutional changes.

For Individuals

Not everyone goes to college. There are also those who do but may not major in public relations or communication and, instead, for instance, may pursue careers in journalism, public affairs, or other fields. As was the case with me, they may even enter the workforce without any forethought of becoming a spokesman. Then, as time passes, circumstances may push them in that direction or they may even become interested in switching to such a career. Thus, they find themselves as the employer's front person with little if any formal training. Do they simply wing it? If not, what can they do to adjust to such a turn of events in their professional lives to begin becoming proficient at this new role? These recommendations are primarily for these types of individuals, as well as to those who have, in fact, set their sights on becoming a press secretary without the proper or formal training.

- Do not operate in a vacuum or allow yourself to be trapped in some kind of self-contained bubble where you are cut off from feedback, input, and even unsolicited sharing. The job of press secretary is one of those where awareness and understanding of as many different and varied perspectives as possible is helpful.
- Make stepping outside yourself a habit. It is not uncommon for writers, such as journalists, to have introverted natures. This does not mean you should not interact and connect with others as regularly as possible. For instance, if you already do have connections with others within your organization, increase them. To be as effective as possible in representing the entire organization, you must know how the world looks from all levels where people sit. The same is true with people external to your organization. It is they to whom you are representing your organization. Get to know them better, too.
- It is never too late to enhance your education. This is true for all of us. If you find yourself elevated to the position of spokesman but lack a formal introduction to public relations, including strategies and theories that help define it, introduce yourself to them. This does not necessarily mean re-enrolling in college. I do suggest introducing yourself to scholars or public relations practitioners to gain a broad knowledge of how communication has evolved to where it is today.
- Contact a spokesman to see if he or she would be willing to let you shadow him or her for a day or two. There is nothing better than sitting at the heels of a person you respect doing what he or she does and then being able to ask direct questions about various choices and actions that person takes. It is invaluable.
- The spokesman's job does not begin and end with the time he or she spends at the podium giving interviews. Those time blocks when you are not giving out statements or being interviewed does not constitute free time. The more time you devote to preparing and maintaining connections with others, the better you will be when you do give public statements or grant interviews.

For Higher Education

Universities and colleges play a vital role in training and preparing individuals to meet the challenges of society. Without question, they have embraced communication and public relations as important fields of study to offer students. Furthermore, the amount of scholarly research, rise of scholarly journals and publications, and high number of professional and academic conferences and seminars are representative of this recognition (Botan & Hazelton, 2006). Collectively, they demonstrate a "next step" in the study of people as complex beings in terms of their behavior and factors that drive or motivate their inter-relations. Communication as a social science examines the relationship between all of us beings regarding how we connect and the reasons behind efforts to connect. Furthermore, public relations speaks to efforts to identify and analyze special strategies used to make those connections and then maintain them.

Thus, given the overriding purposes of communication and public relations as areas of study and potential stepping stones toward careers in those same areas, what can and should universities and colleges do to give the function of organizational spokesman a proper focus? Following are my recommendations:

- The first step is for departments of communication or public relations to establish an academic concentration in organizational or even media spokesmanship. Such action would immediately establish a set road map toward a career in this type of public relations role. Furthermore, it would indicate to prospective employers that students completing this concentration have received focused training.
- A specific academic concentration requires a set or string of specific courses. Such requirements should include courses on communication ethics and behavioral science. The former will direct students in how they should behave, and the latter will give them a better understanding and appreciation of why they and others behave the way they do, particularly in terms of why we communicate the way we do in any given situation.
- While spokesmen do not have to be perfectly articulate, it is important that they be able to speak well. Thus, public speaking should be part of their training and education.
- Communication professors and instructors should adjust each syllabus they design so that students are required at least once each semester to discuss an issue in front of their class and then take questions about it. The instructors can work with students to help them prepare challenging questions and equally challenging topics on which students can present. This kind of dynamic is just as much part of communication as is learning to write press releases, contribute to social media, or devise public relations strategies.
- Departments of communication or public relations should work with various profit and nonprofit organizations to establish internship opportunities for prospective press secretaries. Give them a chance to earn college credit while working with professional spokespeople.

Conclusions

The above recommendations are not meant in any way to provide a definitive answer for establishing a universally accepted road map toward the adequate preparation and training of future press secretaries. Rather, they are designed to help create an awareness that such a road map should be considered by scholars as well as reaffirm the establishment of the organizational spokesman role. In my judgment, while such a role is already well entrenched with no debate of whether such a reality is needed, improvement in the performance and purpose of spokesmanship is needed. All organizations need advocates. All individuals seeking public office need others speaking on their behalf. But, just as much, they need people who are carrying out those charges in ways that strengthen support among their followers and create sincere and respectful dialogue with those who are not. The scholarly community needs to become more actively involved in helping ensure that men and women who aspire to fill such a role in the future are well trained and qualified both in skill and mind-set. Achieving this will be of benefit to us all.

Chapter Highlights

- Institutions of higher learning need to take a more defined and active role in helping provide prospective press secretaries with a clearer path toward achieving these positions.
- The organizational spokesman role has largely been embraced by the public and private sectors.

Discussion Questions

- Do you know people currently serving in a spokesman capacity? How did they achieve their job?
- What steps would you recommend to people wishing to gain work as a spokesman or press secretary?
- What skills do you believe an organizational spokesman should have?

Focus On

Beth Jannery, President of Jannery Communications; Instructor and Coordinator of the Journalism Concentration, Department of Communication, George Mason University; and Author

Beth Jannery founded and has served as the chief executive officer of Jannery Communications since 2000. Her projects in this time have included media work, public relations, marketing, editing, writing, development, and consulting. She has also taught undergraduate courses in public relations, communication, and writing at numerous institutions, including American University in Washington, D.C., Marist College in New York, and currently George Mason University in Fairfax, Virginia. In addition, she has served as director of communication for the Belfer Center for Science and International Affairs at Harvard University's John F. Kennedy School of Government, senior writer and editor at the *Journal of Electronic Defense*, assistant managing writer and editor with *Satellite DIRECT* and *Satellite ORBIT* magazines, and associate writer and editor at Inside Washington Publishers.

She is the creator and author of the Simple Grace nonfiction book series and has two novels in the publishing pipeline: *Finding Grace Again* and *The Admiral's Daughter*.

Jannery earned her undergraduate degree in communication at Framingham State College and her master's degree, also in communication, at Boston University.

Question: We think of press secretaries as the folks who stand in front of the podium and take questions from reporters or give out information to them. But they also work closely with the press in other ways and even help prepare others to speak to the media. Can you talk about these duties?

Answer: The press secretary can serve as a buffer between reporters and a chief officer they may wish to interview. When a journalist goes to the press person with specific questions, it is not unusual that the spokesman may not know the answer. The reporter may then want to talk to a higher-up. The spokesman might know the top officer may not actually want to talk with reporters at that moment, so he or she can do it. They can carry the reporter's questions forward while serving as a buffer between their boss and the press.

It is key for the spokesman to thoroughly understand where the reporter is coming from. They need to know what story the reporter is pursuing so they help facilitate the communication process. This helps their credibility. But the spokesman can damage their credibility if they do not try to cooperate with reporters and help them do their job. Reporters understand that the press secretary may not know all the answers, but they do want to know someone is helping them get their answers. When I worked at Harvard, I always tried to be mindful of what reporters wanted. The bottom line is they wanted a story: theirs and possibly another you might be able to suggest to them. You want them to walk away with having a story.

Question: Would you help your people determine who might be the best person to interview with the press? I ask that as there may be an occasion when just because a reporter asks for a specific person, that does not mean that person is actually the best one to talk with.

Answer: That's right. It is vital the press secretary knows all the key internal players and who is best in interview situations. These interactions do not have to be as high-profile as a press conference. But they are as important as the more visible actions of the press secretary.

Question: What you are describing also plays into the notion that the press secretary sometimes needs to play the role of a reporter and ask their people the hard questions.

Answer: Oh, yes. This happens behind the scenes. You need to think like a journalist. In a special way, the press secretary is a wall. By working with reporters openly and serving as a go-between between the press and the organizations, the press secretary is helping lower that wall or take it down. This includes suggesting story angles to reporters and brainstorming with your people to come up with stories to suggest to reporters.

The best spokesmen are the ones who think like journalists and even see them as collaborators. The worst ones are those that have a "me against you" mentality when working with the press. There is a way that press secretaries can communicate respect and appreciation for the reporters.

People do not automatically start out being a press secretary. There are lots of other jobs they perform on their way to stepping into that position. A number of them are behind-the-scenes in nature. It is not unlike a graduate who wants to become a TV anchorman. While that's great, there are other jobs they need to learn and do before they are ready to sit behind that desk. You need to learn how to edit, report, and write first. There is also a level of professional courtesy that comes into play here. Reporters call, and they expect and deserve to be called back. If this doesn't happen, this damages whatever positive relationship you may be trying to have with them.

Question: Social media is changing the whole spokesman-reporter dynamic.

Answer: Without a doubt that's true. Press secretaries and their peers can no longer control stories like they used to. This means being more flexible and recognizing stories are able to get out through many more avenues than how it used to be. it would be a major mistake for the spokesman to resist this. Whether they like this loss of ironclad control they used to have over what information is released and when it is released, the reality is technology is making it much easier for reporters and even non-reporters to find things out and pass them along to others.

Source: B. Jannery (personal communication, February, 2013).

References

Argenti, P. (2002). Crisis communication: Lessons from 9/11. *Harvard Business Review, 80*(12), 103–109.

Barnard, C. I. (1938). *The functions of the executive.* Cambridge, MA: Harvard University Press.

Barnlund, D. C. (2008). A transactional model of communication. In C. D. Mortensen (Ed.), *Communication theory* (pp.47–57). New Brunswick, NJ: Transition Publishers.

Barton, L. (2001). *Crisis in organizations II* (2nd ed.). Cincinnati, OH: College Divisions South-Western.

Bayles, M. (1989). *Professional ethics.* Belmont, CA: Wadsworth.

Berger, A. (1995). *Essentials of mass communication theory.* London: Sage Publications.

Berkowtiz, D., & Adams, D. B. (1990). Information subsidy and agenda-building in television news. *Journalism Quarterly, 64,* 508–513.

Bernays, E. (1923). *Crystallizing public opinion.* New York: Boni and Liveright.

Block, P. (1993). *Stewardship: Choosing service over self-interest.* San Francisco: Berrett-Koehler.

Botan, C. H. (2006). Grand strategy, strategy and tactics in public relations. In C. H. Botan & V. Hazelton (Eds.), *Public relations theory II.* New York: Lawrence Erlbaum Associates.

Botan, C. H., & Taylor, M. (2005). The role of trust in channels of strategic communication for building civil society. *Journal of Communication, 54*(4), 685–702.

Buzzawell, P. M., & Stohl, C. (1999). The Redding tradition of organizational communication scholarship: W. Charles Redding and his legacy, *Communication Studies, 50*(4), 324–336.

Cappela, J. N. (1983). Conversational involvement: Approaching and avoiding others. In J. M. Wieman & R. P. Harrison (Eds.), *Nonverbal interaction* (pp. 113–148). Beverly Hills, CA: Sage Publications.

Carney, A., & Jorden, A. (1993). Prepare for business-related crises. *Public Relations Journal, 49,* 34–35.

Censer, J. R. (2010). *On the trail of the D.C. sniper.* Charlottesville: University of Virginia Press.

Central Hudson Gas and Electrical Corporation v. Public Service Commission of New York, 447 US 557, 100 S. Ct. 2343.

Chernow, R. (1998). *Titan: The life of John D. Rockefeller Sr.* New York: Random House.

Childers, L. C., & Grunig, J. (1999). *Guidelines for measuring relationships in public relations.* Gainesville, FL: Institute for Public Relations.

Conrad, C. (1993). *The ethical nexus: Values, communication and organizational decisions.* Norwood, NJ: Ablex.

Coombs, W. T. (1999). *Ongoing crisis communication.* London: Sage Publications.

Coombs, W. T. (2006). Crisis management: A communicative approach. In C. H. Botan & V. Hazelton (Eds.), *Public Relations Theory II.* New York: Lawrence Erlbaum Associates.

Coombs, W. T. (2007a). Crisis management and communication. *Institute for Public Relations,* October, 1–17.

Coombs, W. T. (2007b). *Ongoing crisis communication: Planning, managing, and responding* (2nd ed.). Thousand Oaks, CA: Sage Publications.

Crable, R. E. (1990). "Organizational rhetoric" as the fourth great system: Theoretical, critical, and pragmatic implications. *Journal of Applied Communication Research, 18*(2), 115–128.

Crable, R. E., & Vibbert, S. L. (1986). *Public relations as communication management.* Edna, MN: Bellwether Press.

--Crabtree, J. (2011). *The importance of community relationships between small businesses and the community.* Senior Project, California Polytechnic State University, San Luis Obispo.

Cutlip, S. (1995). *Public relations history from the 17th to the 20th century.* New York: Lawrence Erlbaum Associates.

--Cutlip, S., & Center, A. H. (1952). *Effective public relations.* Englewood Cliffs, NJ: Prentice Hall.

Cutlip, S., Center, A. H., & Broom, G. (1985) (1985 & 1994). *Effective public relations.* Englewood Cliffs, NJ: Prentice Hall.

D'Alessandro, D. F. (1991). Image building: Why is it so difficult? In M. P. McEleath & P. W. Miller (Eds.), *Introduction to public relations and advertising: A reader from the consumer's point of view.* Needham Heights, MA: Ginn Press.

David, G. (2011). Internal communication—Essential component of crisis communication. *Journal of Media Research, 4*(2), 72–81.

Davis, K. (1973). The case for and against business assumption of social responsibilities. *Academy of Management Journal, 16,* 312–322.

Deatherage, C. P., & Hazelton, V. (1998). Effects of organizational worldviews on the practice of public relations: A test of the theory of public relations excellence. *Journal of Public Relations, 10*(1), 57–71.

Deetz, S. (1982). Critical interpretive research in organizational communication. *Western Journal of Speech Communication, 46,* 131–149.

Edmondson, V. C. (2006). Organizational surveys: A system for employee voice. *Journal of Applied Communication Research, 34*(4), 307–310.

Ellis, D. G. (1979). An analysis of relational communication in ongoing group systems. Unpublished doctoral dissertation, University of Utah, Salt Lake City.

Entman, R. M. (1993). Framing: Toward a clarification of a fractured paradigm. *Journal of Communication, 43,* 51–58.

Escudero, V., & Rogers, L. (Eds.). (2004). *Relational communication: An interactional perspective to the study of process and form.* Mahwah, NJ: Lawrence Erlbaum Associates.

Ewen, S. (2006). *PR! A social history of spin.* New York: Basic Books.

Fairhurst, G. T., & Putnam, L. L. (1998). Reflections on the organization-communication equivalency question: The contributions of James Taylor and his colleagues. *The Communication Review, 3,* 1–19.

Fearn-Banks, K. (2007). *Crisis communication: A casebook approach.* Mahwah, NJ: Lawrence Erlbaum Associates.

Fehrenbacher, D. E. (1960). The origins and purpose of Lincoln's "house divided" speech. *Mississippi Historical Review, 46*(4), 615–643.

Fink, S. (1986). *Crisis management: Planning for the Inevitable.* New York: AMACOM.

Fitzpatrick, K. R. (1996). Public relations and the law: A survey of practitioners. *Public Relations Review,* 1–8.

Foner, P. S. (1980). *History of the labor movement in the United States: The AFL in the progressive era, 1910–1915.* New York: International Publishers.

Fukuyama, F. (1995). *Trust: The social virtues and creation of prosperity.* New York: Free Press.

Gandy, O. H. (1982). *Beyond agenda setting: Information subsidies and public policy.* Norwood, NJ: Ablex.

Gilligan, C. (1982). *In a different voice: Physiological theory and women's development.* Cambridge, MA: Harvard University Press.

Giuliani, R. (2002). *Leadership.* New York: Miramax Books.

Goffman, E. (1974). *Frame analysis: An essay on the organization of experience.* Cambridge, MA: Harvard University Press.

--Goodman, M. (1998). *Corporate communications for executives.* Albany: State University of New York Press.

Gornter, H. F. (1991). *Ethics for public managers.* London: Praeger.

Grunig, J. (1983). Basic research provides knowledge that makes evaluation possible. *Public Relations Quarterly, 28,* 28–32.

Grunig, J. E. (1989). Symmetrical presuppositions as a framework for public relations theory. In C. Botan & V. Hazelton (Eds.), *Public relations theory.* Hillsdale, NJ: Lawrence Erlbaum Associates.

Grunig, J., Grunig, L., & Dozier, D. M. (2002). *Excellent public relations and effective organizations: A study of communication management in three countries.* Mahwah, NJ: Lawrence Erlbaum Associates.

Grunig, J. E., & Hunt, T. (1984). *Managing public relations.* New York: Holt, Rinehart and Winston.

Guth, D. W., & Marsh, C. (2012). *Public relations: A values-driven approach.* Boston: Allyn & Bacon.

Hackman, M. Z., & Johnson, C.E. (2009). *Leadership: A communication perspective.* Long Grove, IL: Waveland Press, Inc.

Hallahan, K. (1999). Seven models of framing: Implications for public relations. *Journal of Public Relations Research, 11*, 205–242.

Harkin, R. (2008). *Navigating the legal minefield of private investigators, detectives and security police.* New York: Looseleaf Law Publications.

Hayes, D. C., Hendrix, J. A., & Kumar, P. D. (2013). *Public relations cases.* Boston: Wadsworth Cengage Learning.

Hearit, K. M. (1994). Apologies and public relations crisis at Chrysler, Toshiba, and Volvo. *Public Relations Review, 20*(2), 113–125.

Heinaman, R. (1995). *Aristotle and moral realism.* Boulder, CO: Westview Press.

Hendrix, J. A., & Hayes, D. C. (2007). *Public relations cases.* Belmont, CA: Thomson & Wadsworth.

Hermann, C. F. (1963). Some consequences of crisis which limit the viability of organizations. *Administrative Science Quarterly, 8*, 61–82.

Hersey, P. (1984). *The situational leader.* Escondido, CA: Center for Leadership Studies.

Hiebert, R. E. (1966). *Courtier to the crowd: The story of Ivy Lee and the development of public relations.* Ames: Iowa State University Press.

Hill, I. (1980). *Common sense and everyday ethics.* Washington, D.C.: Ethics Resource Center.

--Hill, J. W. (1963). *The making of a public relations man.* New York: David McKay.

Huber, J., & Boyle, P. (2005). Roche's holistic approach to leadership communication: Clarifying communication roles and responsibilities for leaders. *Strategic Communication Management, 9*(6), 18–21.

Huttenstine, M. (1993). New roles, new problems, new concerns, new laws. *Southern Public Relations Journal, 1*(1), 5.

Ihlen, O. (2010). Love in touch times: Crisis communication and public relations, *The Review of Communication, 10*(2), 98–111.

Jones, J. P. (1955). Organization for public relations. In E. L. Bernays (Ed.), *The engineering of consent* (pp. 156–184). Norman: University of Oklahoma Press.

Jordan, J. M. (1993). Executive cognitive control in communication extending plan-based theory. *Human Communication Research, 25*(1), 5–38.

Katz, E. (1957). The two-step flow of communication: An up-to-date report on a hypothesis. *Public Opinion Quarterly, 21*(1), 61–78.

Kelly, K. S. (1991). *Fundraising and public relations: A critical analysis.* Hillsdale, NJ: Lawrence Erlbaum Associates.

Kennen, W. R., & Hazelton, V. (2006). Internal public relations, social capital, and the role of effective organizational communication. In C. H. Botan & V. Hazelton (Eds.), *Public relations theory II.* New York: Lawrence Erlbaum Associates.

Koten, J. A. (1986). Moving toward higher standards for American business. *Public Relations Review, 12*(3), 3.

--Krone, K. (2005). Trends in organizational communication research: Sustaining the discipline, sustaining ourselves. *Communication Studies, 56*(1), 95–105.

Krone, K., & Morgan, J. (2000). Becoming deeply multi-perspectical: Commentary on finding common ground in organizational communication research. In S. Corman & M. S. Poole (Eds.), *Perspectives on organizational communication: Finding common ground* (pp. 144–151). New York: Guilford Press.

Kruckeberg, D., & Starck, K. (2000). *The role and ethics of commercial building for consumer products and services.* Paper presented at the convention of the National Communication Association, Seattle, Washington.

Kruckeberg, D., Starck, K., & Vujnovic, M. (2006). The role and ethics of community-building for consumer products and services. In C. H. Botan & V. Hazleton (Eds.), *Public relations theory II.* New York: Lawrence Erlbaum Associates.

--Kunhardt, P. (1999). *Gerald R. Ford: Healing the nation.* New York: Riverhead Books.

Lang, G. E., & Lang, K. (1981). Watergate: An exploration of the agenda-building process. *Mass Communication Review Yearbook, 2,* 447–469.

Leanna, C. R., & Van Buren III, H. J. (1999). Organizational social capital and employment practices. *Academy of Management Review, 24*(3), 538–555.

Ledingham, J. A. (2000). *Relationship management: Where do we go from here?* Paper presented at the Annual Convention of the International Communication Association, Acapulco, Mexico.

Ledingham, J. A., & Bruning, S. D. (2000a). Background and current trends in the study of relationship management. In J. A. Ledingham & S. D. Bruning (Eds.), *Public relations as relationship management: A relational approach to the study and practice of public relationsi do not know page numbers.* Mahwah, NJ: Lawrence Erlbaum Associates.

Ledingham, J. A., & Bruning, S. D. (Eds.). (2000b). *Public relations as relationship management: A relational approach to the study and practice of public relations.* Mahwah, NJ: Lawrence Erlbaum Associates.

Lerbinger, O. (1997). *The crisis manager: Facing risk and responsibility.* Mahwah, NJ: Lawrence Erlbaum Associates.

Levy, C. S. (1974). On the development of a code of ethics. *Social Work, 19,* 207–216.

Lewin, K., Lippett, R., & White, R. K. (1939). Patterns of aggressive behavior in experimentally created "social climates." *Journal of Social Psychology, 10,* 271–299.

Lorch, R. S. (1978). *Public administration.* St. Paul, this is correctMN: West.

--MacDougall, C. D. (1952). *Understanding public opinion.* New York: Macmillan.

Macnamara, J. (2005). PR metrics: How to measure public relations and corporate communications. In C. Tymson & P. Lazar (Eds.), *The new Australian & New Zealand public relations manual.* Sydney, Australia: Tymson Communications.

Martin, W. P., & Singletary, M. W. (1981). Newspaper treatment of state government releases. *Journalism Quarterly, 58,* 93–96.

Maslow, A. (1954). *Motivation and personality.* New York: Harper & Row.

McCombs, M. E., & Shaw, D. L. (1972). The agenda setting function of mass media. *Public Opinion Quarterly, 69,* 813–824.

McGregor, D. (1960). *The human side of enterprise.* Boston: Harvard University Press.

McIntyre, J. (2009). Off the record. *American Journalism Review, www.ajr.org.,* April/May.

McMaster, M. D. (1996). *The intelligence advantage: Organizing for complexity.* Newton, MA: Butterworth-Heinemann.

~~McPhee, R. D., & Tompkins, P. K. (1986). *Organizational communication: Traditional themes and new directions.* Thousand Oaks, CA: Sage Publications.

Michaelson, D., & Macleod, S. (2007). The application of "best practices" in public relations measurement and evaluation systems. *Public Relations Journal, 2*(1), 1–14.

Miller, G. R. (1989). Persuasion and public relations: Two "Ps" in a pod. In C. H. Botan & V. Hazelton, Jr. (Eds.), *Public relations theory* (pp. 45–66). Hillsdale, NJ: Lawrence Erlbaum Associates.

Miller, M. D., & Levine, T. R. (1996). Persuasion. In M. B. Sawen & D. W. Stacks (Eds.), *An integrated approach to communication theory and research.* Mahwah, NJ: Lawrence Erlbaum Associates.

Montgomery, D. (1983). A Texan meets the press (and says a little prayer). *Fort Worth Star Telegram,* p. 29A.

Moore, L. P., & Warren, J. (1992). News elements and editors' choices, *Public Relations Review, 18,* 47–53.

Morgan, G. (1998). *Images of organizations.* Thousand Oaks, CA: Sage Publications.

Nagel, J. H. (1991). Psychological obstacles to administrative responsibility: Lessons of the MOVE disaster. *Policy Analysis and Management, 10*(1), 1–23.

Newsom, D., Turk, J. V., & Kruckeberg, D. (2013). *This is PR: The realities of public relations.* Boston: Wadsworth.

The New York Times Company v. Sullivan, 376 US 255, 270 (1964).

Northouse, P. (2007). *Leadership: Theory and practice* (4th ed.). Thousand Oaks, CA: Sage Publications.

Okay, A., & Okay, A. (2008). The place of theory in public relations practice. In T. L. Hansen-Horn & B. D. Neff (Eds.), *Public relations: From theory to practice.* Fort Worth, TX: Harcourt Brace College Publishers.

Organ, D. W. (2004). Linking pins between organizations and environment: Individuals do the interacting. *Business Horizons, 14*(6), 73–80.

Page, N., & Czuba, C. E. (1999). Empowerment: What is it? *Journal of Extension, 37*(5), 1–6.

Partington, A. (2002). The Linguistics of Political Argrument, the Spin Doctor and the Wolf Pack at the White House, New York: Routledge.

Pauchart, T. C., & Mitroff, I. I. (1992). *Transforming the crisis-prone organizations.* San Francisco: Jossey-Bass.

Pfau, M., & Wan, H. (2006). Persuasion: An intrinsic function of public relations. In C. H. Botan & V. Hazelton (Eds.), *Public relations theory II.* New York: Lawrence Erlbaum Associates.

Philadelphia Special Investigation Commission. (1986). *Conclusions and recommendations.* City of Philadelphia, PA

Phillips, B. (2011). *Nine practical tips for a spokesman.* Retrieved from www.prdaily.com.

Pimlott, J. A. (1951). *Public relations and American democracy.* Princeton, NJ: Princeton University Press.

Portest, A. (1998). Social capital: Its origins and applications in modern sociology. *Annual Review of Sociology, 22,* 1–25.

Pratt, C. B. (2006). Reformulating the emerging theory of corporate social responsibility as good governance. In C. H. Botan & V. Hazelton (Eds.), *Public relations theory II*. New York: Lawrence Erlbaum Associates.

Public Relations Society of America. (2000). Ethical Guidance for Public Relations Practitioners. *PRSA member code of ethics*. www.prsa.org/about PRSA/ethics.

Public Relations Society of America (2012). What is Public Relations? www/prsa.org/about PRSA/ pubic relations defined.

Redding, W. C. (1972). *Communication within the organization*. New York: Industrial Communication and Purdue University.

Rockland, D. B. 2006). Asked to calculate ROI? Don't sweat it—Just ask good questions from the get-go. *Public Relations Tactics, July*. I do not know page numbers or volume #

Rogers, L. E. (1972). *Relational communication control coding manual*. Unpublished manuscript, University of Utah, Salt Lake City, UT.

Roosevelt, T. R. (1910). *Citizenship in a republic*.speech, Paris, France (4/23/1910).

Roussel, P. (2006). A press secretary's prayer, by one who's been there. Chron.com. 4/21.

Rowan, K. E. (1991). Goals, obstacles and strategies in risk communication. *Journal of Applied Communication Research, 19, (4), 300–329*.

Sandman, P. M. (1983). *Responding to community outrage: Strategies for effective risk communication*. Paper presented at the meeting of the American Industrial Hygiene Association, Fairfax, Virginia.

Sandman, P. M., & Miller, P. (1991). *Outrage and technical detail: The impact of agency behavior on community risk perception*. Trenton: New Jersey Department of Environmental Protection.

Schlesinger, A. M., Jr. (1945). *The age of Jackson*. New York: Back Bay Books.

Seeger, M. W., Vennette, S., Ulmer, R. R., & Sellnow, T. L. (2002). Patterns of media use, information seeking, and reported needs in post-crisis contexts. In B. Greenberg (Ed.), *Communication and terrorism* (pp. 53–63). Cresswell, NJ: Hampton Press.

Seifert, W. (1984). Interview. In F. P. Seitel, *The practice of public relations*. Toronto: Charles E. Merrill Publishing Company.

Seitel, F. P. (1984). *The practice of public relations*. Toronto: Charles E. Merrill Publishing Company.

Simon, M. J. (1978, August 29). Speech to North Texas chapter of the Public Relations Society of America,Fort Worth, Texas.

--Smith, R. D. (2009). *Strategic planning for public relations*. New York: Routledge.

Snyder, M. L. (1987). *Public appearances/private realities: The psychology of self-monitoring*. New York: Freeman.

Starck, K., & Kruckeberg, D. (2001). Public relations and community: A reconstructed theory revisited. In R. L. Heath (Ed.), *Handbook of public relations* (pp. 51–59). Thousand Oaks, CA: Sage Publications.

Starks, G. L. (2006, Winter). Managing conflict in public organizations. *The Public Manager*, 55–60.

Steel, R. (1966, September 2). Public relations men stress professionalism. *St. Petersburg Times*.

Stillman, R. J. (2005). *Public administration: Concepts and cases*. Boston: Houghton Mifflin Company.

Stovall, J. G. (2012). *Writing for the mass media*. Boston: Pearson.

Sturges, D. L. (1994). Communicating through crisis: A strategy for organizational survival. *Management Communication Quarterly, 7*, 297–316.

Taylor, F. W. (1911). *The principles of scientific management*. New York: Harper Brothers.

Taylor, M., & Kent, M. L. (2007). Taxonomy of mediated crisis responses. *Public Relations Review, 33*, 140–146.

Tedlow, R. S. (1979). *Keeping the corporate image: Public relations and business, 1900–1950*. Greenwich, CT: JAI Press, Inc.

terHorst, J. (1974). *Gerald R. Ford and the future of the presidency*. New York: The Third Press.

Theus, K. T. (1993). Organizations and the media structure of miscommunication. *Management Communication Quarterly, 7*(1), 67–94.

Thompson, J. D., & McEwen, W. J. (1958). Organizational goals and environment: Goal setting as an interaction process. *American Sociological Review, 23*, 23–31.

Trist, E. (1981). *The evolution of sociotechnical systems: A conceptual framework and an action research program* (Occasional Paper No. 2). Toronto: Ontario Quality of Working Life Center.

Vecchi, G. M. (2009, Winter). Conflict & crisis communication: Methods of crisis intervention and stress management. *Annuals of American Psychotherapy Association, 12*(4), 54–63.

Walsch, D. (2011). *A strategic communication approach to crisis situations: A cast study analysis of transformative events at George Mason University and Northern Illinois University*. Fairfax, VA: George Mason University.

Watson, K. M. (1982). An analysis of communication patterns: A method for discriminating leader and member roles. *Academy of Management Journal, 25*, 107–120.

Gerth, H. H. & Mills, C. W. (Eds.) (1946). Essays in Sociology. New York: Oxford University Press. Weber, M. (1946). Max Weber. In H. H. Gerth & C. W. Mills (Eds.). New York: Oxford University Press.

Werth, B. (2006). *31 days: The crisis that gave us the government we have today*. New York: Doubleday.

Wilcox, D. L., & Reber, B. H. (2013). *Public relations writing and media techniques*. Upper Saddle River, NJ: Pearson Education, Inc.

Wilkinson, J. S., Grant, A. E., & Fisher, D. J. (2013). *Principles of convergent journalism*. New York: Oxford University Press.

Wise, G. (1980). *American historical explanations: A strategy for grounded Inquiry*. Minneapolis: University of Minnesota.

Zinn, H. (1990). *The politics of history*. Urbana: University of Illinois Press.

Zoch, L. M., & Molleda, J. (2006). Building a theoretical model of media relations using framing, information subsidies, and agenda-building. In C. H. Botan & V. Hazelton (Eds.), *Public relations theory II* (pp.279 - 310). New York: Lawrence Erlbaum Associates.

About the Author

Daniel L. Walsch has been part of the communication field for more than 40 years as a journalist, public relations practitioner, press secretary, speech writer, university instructor, and author. His most recent books are *A Strategic Communication Approach to Crisis Situation: A Case Study Analysis of Transformative Events at George Mason University and Northern Illinois University*, published in 2011 by Lambert Academic Publishing, and *Communication Wars: Our Perpetual Internal Conflict*, published in 2012 by Cognella, Inc. He maintains a blog, *Why Communication Matters* (www.myskeets.blogspot.com) and is an accredited public relations professional as certified by the Public Relations Society of America. He has graduate degrees in communication and administration and earned his doctorate in communication at George Mason University. Dr. Walsch resides with his wife in Fairfax, Virginia.

CPSIA information can be obtained at www.ICGtesting.com
Printed in the USA
LVOW03s0931030114

367819LV00007B/79/P